SAIVA SIDDHANTA HINDUISM

IN THE LIGHT OF CHRISTIANITY

By

Bramwell Christopher Devaratnam Mather

B.D., Serampore, India, 1932

THESIS

Submitted in the Department of Theology in partial

fulfillment for the requirements of the

degree of

Master of Arts

Pacific School of Religion

May, 1953

Copyright © 1953 Pacific School of Religion, Berkley, California
Copyright © 2013 Ranjini Woodhouse (née Mather)

All rights reserved, including the right to reproduce this book or any portion thereof in any form. No part of the book may be reproduced or transmitted in any form or by any means, electronic or mechanical, including photocopying, recording, or by any information storage or retrieval system without the written permission of the Pacific School of Religion, Berkley, California.

First published by: Pacific School of Religion, USA
Date: 1953

Second Publication by: Souljourney Publishing, United Kingdom
Date: November 2013

ISBN: 978-0-9570251-2-7

Cover design: Original cover design 1953

SAIVA SIDDHANTA HINDUISM

IN THE LIGHT OF CHRISTIANITY

By

Bramwell Christopher Devaratnam Mather

B.D., Serampore, India, 1932

ACKNOWLEDGEMENTS

A special thank you to my daughter Zoë for research she did on her grandfather and finding the information about the existence of the thesis written for his Master of Arts degree.

I am grateful to the Dean of the Pacific School of Religion Mr Bernard Schlager, PhD Dean, PSR, and Mr. David Stiver, Special Collections Librarian, Graduate Theological Union, for making this thesis available to me.

Prue Draper, Historian, The Cotati Historical Society for the information provided on the Dimpfl Ranch and Ludwig Dimpfl and his sister Josefina Dimpfl with whom my father stayed during his time in California.

A special thank you to my son James for taking the time to set up the manuscript in its original format for printing.

My husband John for financing the publication of my Dad's thesis.

In loving memory and heartfelt gratitude;

for the life of my father
BRAMWELL CHRISTOPHER DEVARATNAM MATHER
26 November 1905 - 13 May 1990

And my mother
JANE NAVAMANI MATHER (NÉE SIVAGURU)
17 December 1913 - 22 January 1999

A great inspiration to my father.

Preface

My original intention was to make a study of the three major religions of Ceylon: Buddhism, Hinduism and Islam in the light of Christianity. But it was too big a task to be completed in a short time. So I have confined myself to the study of Saiva Siddhanta Hinduism which is the religion of the vast majority of the people of North Ceylon from which I come.

The technical words used in the thesis take the Tamil form and not the Sanskrit form.

It seems best to acquaint the reader at the outset with the meanings of certain words used in the text so that when he comes to those words he may have a better understanding of them.

<u>Anava</u> is ignorance.

<u>Malam</u> is impurity.

<u>Lingam</u> is the symbol of the male generative organ.

<u>Yoni</u> is the symbol of the female generative organ.

<u>Pati</u> is president or lord.

<u>Pasu</u> is the Soul or bound one.

<u>Pasam</u> is the cord that binds the soul.

TABLE OF CONTENTS

Chapter		Page
I.	Introduction..................................	1- 4
II.	Age of Saivism...............................	5-12
III.	Religion and Worship in the Vedas..........	13-18
IV.	Saiva Siddhanta Hinduism....................	19-26
V.	God in Saiva Siddhanta......................	27-38
VI.	Soul in Saiva Siddhanta.....................	39-47
VII.	Karma in Saiva Siddhanta....................	48-53
VIII.	Deliverance, Grace, Guru in Saiva Siddhanta.............................	54-65
IX.	Light Amidst Darkness.......................	66-75
X.	Jesus Christ the Light of the World........	76-90
	Bibliography................................	91-93

CHAPTER I

INTRODUCTION

Hinduism

Hinduism is the oldest of the world's great faiths. Its literature is traceable to a point of time long anterior to Aristotle and Plato and Socrates, Isaiah and Solomon, Zoroaster, the composition of the Iliad, the fall of Troy -- so carrying the beginnings of its earliest books to at least the period of Israel's captivity in Egypt, if not up to the time of Hammurabi.

Hinduism in its various forms is the religion of over 245 millions of people, and countless numbers have lived and died in it, finding in its many sidedness solace and strength for the world that now is and hope for that which is to be. It is the religion of knowledge; its philosophy is subtle. It is a religion of ritual; its wealth of ceremonies is enormous. Its susceptibility to adaptation is amazing. There is a higher Hinduism of the Philosopher and a Hinduism of the man in the street. In its aspirations after universality it has been found to make itself elastic enough to embrace such striking contrasts as well nigh imperil all claims to consistency. Hinduism is professed from the Himalayas to Cape Comorin and southwards in Ceylon especially in the northern and eastern provinces. It is the religion of the many in these places and the philosophy of the few in the countries of the Occident. Macnicol quotes from Sir Alfred Lyall's Asiatic Studies where the latter compares Hinduism to "a troubled sea without shore or visible horizon, driven to and fro by the winds of boundless credulity and grotesque invention."[1] Whereas Rakhakrishnan calls Hinduism "a subtly unified mass of spiritual thought and realisation."[2] It accepts, he says, "all religious notions as facts and arranges them in the order of their more or less intrinsic significance."[3] Where one sees confusion the other sees order and where one sees only credulity the other sees faith.

The Vedanta system of Hinduism is based on Sanskrit literature and has been studied by Oriental and Occidental scholars. This system was first made famous by Sankara, who lived about 788 A.D. to 850 A.D. He was the supreme Acharya of the Vedantic school. "His fame rests on his commentaries on the Vedanta sutras, the Bhagavad Gita and the chief Upanishads. He held that the true Vedanta system was 'advaita,' i.e. an unqualified monism. Nothing is real except Brahma. Man's soul is the eternal spirit whole and undivided;

---

[1] Nicol Macnicol, Living Religions of the Indian People (London: Student Christian Movement Press, 1934), p. 26.

[2] S. Radhakrishnan, The Hindu View of Life (London: George Allen & Unwin, Ltd., 1927), p. 21.

[3] Ibid., p. 31.

and the world is Maya, illusion. Henceforward the central school of the Vedanta is Advaita -- strictly monistic."[3]

A comparatively little known system is called the Saiva Siddhanta. Max Müller says "In the South of India there exists a philosophical literature which though it shows clear traces of Sanskrit influence, contains also original indigenous elements of great beauty and of great importance for historical purposes. Unfortunately, few scholars only have taken up as yet the study of the Dravidian languages and literature, but young students who complain that there is nothing left to do in Sanskrit Literature would, I believe, find their labour amply rewarded in that field." The Rev. G. U. Pope who was a Missionary in India was a great and keen student of the Tamil language and he translated some of the Tamil classics into English. In his introduction to the translation of Tiruvasagam he says "The Civa Siddhanta system is the most elaborate, influential and undoubtedly the most intrinsically valuable of all the religions of India. It is peculiarly the South Indian and Tamil religion and must be studied by every one who hopes to understand and influence the great South Indian peoples. Çaivism is the old prehistoric religion of South India essentially existing from pre-Aryan times and holds sway over the hearts of the Tamil people."[4]

---

[3] J. N. Farquhar, *A Primer of Hinduism* (London: Oxford University Press, 1912), p. 118.

[4] G. U. Pope, *Tiruvachagam* (tr.) (Oxford: Clarendon Press, 1900), p. lxxiv.

It is to the study of this system of Hinduism that we now turn our attention.

CHAPTER II

THE AGE OF SAIVISM

Meaning of the Word Siddhanta.--Tamil writers use both the Tamil form 'Siddhantam' and the Sanskrit 'Siddhanta.' The word means 'sure end,' 'assured result,' 'correct conclusion,' (the true end' or the 'ultimate goal.' Certain astronomical works are called Siddhantas. The word as applied to religious philosophy has the content of a 'mathematical finding,' 'a logical conclusion,' "a true end.' Hence it is the popular teaching that Siddhanta means 'the true end,' 'the ultimate goal.' Siddhanta is the accomplished end 'fixed or established truth.'

Saiva Siddhanta is the theology of the Hindus who worship the God Siva. Their theology is based on the Vedas, but they have other sacred scriptures as authoritative.

> Hinduism is a group of religions which accept the authority of the Vedas. Each member of the group has an authority of its own, which the Vedas supplement, and in the light of which they are interpreted. The most important members of this group are Saivism, Vaishnavism, and Shaktaism, whose additional authority are respectively are respectively the Siva-agamas, the Pancharatra and the Shakta-agamas. In spite of their akinness, they differ widely in their philosophies and ceremonials. Of these three religions Saivism has the largest number of followers both in India and in Ceylon. In its orthodox form it is found in South India, Ceylon, Kashmir and

Nepal. Shaktaism is concentrated in Bengal, the capital of which, Calcutta, is named after Kali, a name of Shakti."[1]

The Age of Saivism.--"Reference is made to Saivism and the Siva-Agamas in the Mahabharata."[2] This reference by itself does not give antiquity to Saivism as the "composition of the epic as we have it is generally ascribed to the period from the second century B.C. to the second century A.D., although its beginnings may go back to 400 B.C. and its amplification probably continued till A.D. 400 and even later."[3] But there are other reasons for claiming antiquity for Saivism.

Race Movements.--Scholars who have studied the movements of race affecting India are persuaded that there are several elements present and find Negrito, Mongoloid and other strains. It is also claimed that a group called the Proto-Australoid seems to have come from the West. Many of these still survive in the aboriginal peoples of India but a branch of them passed on to Australia in very ancient times. Finally we have the Nordic Aryan speaking group who were until fairly recent times thought to be the beginning of Indian history and culture. There is abundance of evidence to show that this group brought vocabularies related to early Mediterranean languages. There

---

[1] S. Shivapadasundaram, The Saiva School of Hinduism (London: G. Allen & Unwin, Ltd., 1934), p. 13.

[2] Ibid.

[3] Jack Finegan, The Archeology of World Religions (Princeton: Princeton University Press, 1952), p. 153.

are many words common to the Aryan language of India and the Greek and Roman languages of Europe. It is believed by many scholars that the Mohenjo-Daro people spoke a primitive Dravidian language. Among the Dravidian elements of their civilization was to be found the worship of Siva and the practise of the Yoga system.

The Indus Valley is one of the important agricultural areas of India. It is the valley in which the five great rivers carry the melting snows of the Himalayas into the Indus river. Hence it is subject to floods which bring large alluvial soil deposits which in turn often change the course of the rivers burying cities on their way. It was down the Indus that Alexander's great army marched on its way out of India.

Scholarship has long been familiar with the history of the civilizations of the Sumer, Akkad, Babylon, Egypt, Assyria and other hands. Excavations during the past century have brought to light many facts concerning these lands. There were no such remains of former civilizations in India before the coming of the Aryans in 1500 B.C. But in 1862 with the formation of an archeological department under General Alexander Cunningham as Surveyor, archeological interest in that area was established. In 1922-23 Mr. R. D. Banerji, excavating in the Buddhist Stupa in Mohenjo-daro, came across some inscribed seals with pictographic characters which were like some that had been discovered at Harappa (about 400 miles further north) in the Punjab a few years earlier. It was not until two years after this that further excavations by Sir John Marshall at Mohenjo-daro convinced him that both these places revealed a much older civilization than had been known before.

Ernest Mackay in his Early Indus Civilization reports three periods during which the various cities were built on this one site, each divided into three or four phases. It is estimated that the civilization dated from 2800 B.C. to 2500 B.C., a period of 300 years. These dates have been agreed on because of similarities in findings in Sumeria as well as in Mohenjo-daro.[4] The remains in Mohenjo-daro and Harrappa reveal ruins of cities of considerable size and of a high state of civilization. Laid out in regular streets, with houses of large as well as small size, and with walls, pavements, drainage wells, etc., the inhabitants must have possessed a high degree of the science of building and city making.

Religion.--It is most interesting to find that quite contrary to the fact that India had been so religious since the days of the Vedas (about 1500 B.C.) no very clear evidence regarding religion in the Indus Valley has as yet been discovered. There are no buildings that can be clearly recognized as meant for religious purposes. Nor have any relics,

---

[4] Ernest Mackay, Early Indus Civilizations (London: Luzac and Co., Ltd., 1948), pp. 146-155.

shrines or altars been found and no objects that could be said to belong to religious cults. What little evidence there is would seem to point to the recognition of a Mother-Goddess. There are figurines of terra-cotta of standing females, semi-nude, some smoke stained, perhaps from burning oil before the figure. One seal shows the figure of a man with a sickle and a woman seated on the ground with hands raised in supplication, probably suggesting human sacrifice.

There is the figure of a three-faced male wearing a horned head-dress, showing phallic traditions and surrounded by an elephant and other animals. In this there are several ideas connected with the worship of Siva in later days. These include the trimukha (three faces), lingam, and Pasu Pati (Lord of Animals). It might also include the idea of Yoga. There are a large number of relics suggesting that this deity together with the Mother-Goddess was popular. These include yonic and phallic stones of various sizes which were probably symbolic of fertility. There are also small ring-stones suggestive of yoni which is closely connected with the lingam, but this is not clearly proven yet. There is evidence of zoolatry indicated by the association of the bull with Siva on various seals. Even today the bull is the Vahana (vehicle) on which Siva travels.[5]

---

[5] Mackay, op. cit., pp. 52-76.

Finegan sums up pre-Aryan religion thus:

> There appears to have been much animism in the religion of the Indus civilization, and there is evidence for the worship of trees and animals as well as for cults of baetylic and phallic stones ... If both a mother goddess and a prototypal Siva were worshipped, then the people of the Indus valley had advanced from dynamistic and animistic foundations to the creation of distinctive aspects of India's historical polytheism.[6]

Authors of the Indus Civilization.--It is fairly generally admitted now that the people who lived in the Indus valley about 3000 B.C. were Dravidians.[7] These Dravidians were probably of Mediterranean origin. This seems more clearly shown by the languages than by the theories of race and skull measurements. At one time it was thought that all elements of higher culture that had been found in India were due to Aryan invaders of about 1500 B.C. but it is now believed that in many ways the civilization of the Indus valley was far superior to the village civilization of the Aryans. The pre-Aryans of Mohenjo-daro were certainly in possession of a higher material culture than that which the seminomadic Aryans could show. Certainly no ruins comparable with those of the Indus valley have been found belonging to the Aryans.

There are, on the other hand, similarities to Sumeria,

---

[6] Jack Finegan, The Archeology of World Religions (Princeton: Princeton University Press, 1952), pp. 127-28.

[7] Encyclopedia Britannica, Vol. XII (Chicago: Encyclopedia Britannica, Inc., 1952), pp. 164 ff.

Elam, and other countries of Mesopotamia. Among these are the organization of society in cities, the continued but sparing use of stones, with copper and brass for weapons, tools and vessels, picture signs for writing, maces of stone or metal along with spears, daggers, bows and arrows. There was also a high development in the minor arts and crafts such as that of the silver- and goldsmiths. Ornaments of shells and various kinds of stones were also abundant.

It might be well to look at some of the outstanding differences between the earlier Indus valley civilization and the later Vedic. Interestingly enough the Indus civilization was urban as contrasted with the Vedic village civilization. The Vedic had gold, copper bronze, silver and iron, while the Indus had no iron and silver was more common than gold. The Vedic Aryans ate meat but had an aversion to fish, while the Indus people ate fish as a common diet and also other aquatic creatures. The Aryans had horses, but these were unknown to the Indus people. The Aryans prized the cow above all other animals but to the Indus folk the cow had no particular sanctity. Among the Aryans the female element in religion was subordinate to the male, while in the Indus valley the Mother Goddess and Siva were prominent. Among the Aryans phallic worship was abhorrent while in the Indus valley it was common. "Their religion," says Sir John Marshall (about the Indus valley peoples),

> is so characteristically Indian as hardly to be distinguishable from still living

Hinduism or at least from that aspect of it which is bound up with animism and the cultus of Siva and the Mother Goddess -- still the most potent forces in popular worship.[8]

Among the many revelations that Mohenjo-daro and Harrappa have had in store for us, none perhaps is more remarkable than this discovery that Saivism has a history going back to chalcolithic age or perhaps even further still, and that it takes its place as the most ancient living faith in the world.[9]

---

[8] Sir John Marshall, Mohenjo-daro and the Indus Civilization (London: A. Probsthain, 1931), p. vii.

[9] Ibid.

CHAPTER III

RELIGION AND WORSHIP IN THE VEDAS

Since the Saiva Siddhanta claims to be based on the Vedas this chapter is devoted to Religion and Worship in the Vedas. Some authorities would carry us back to 3000 B.C. as the beginning of the Vedic Period. Others mention 2000 or 1500 and some come down to much more recent times. Hopkins is content to say that he thinks that the collection of the Rig Veda was completed by about 800 B.C. but admits that many of the Hymns were written much before that. He says,

> We are unable to admit that either in language or social development or in literary growth more than a few centuries are necessary to account for the whole development of Hindu literature up to the time of Buddha.[1]

Finegan concludes,

> The hymns of the Rig Veda are generally believed to go back to the time from about 1500 to 1000 B.C. and they come down to us in a text which has been transmitted without substantial variation at least since the 6th or 5th century B.C.[2]

---

[1] E. W. Hopkins, *India Old and New* (New Haven: Yale University Press, 1913), p. 6.

[2] J. Finegan, *The Archeology of World Religions* (Princeton: Princeton University Press, 1952), p. 190.

Sir John Marshall reasons that no trace of the Indus civilization remained when the Aryans came to India.

Religion and Worship.--There is a vast difference between the simplicity of worship in the early Vedic religion as shown in the Rig Veda and that of the later period as shown in the Atharva Veda and the Brahmanas.

There is evidence of the worship of many gods in the Rig Veda period -- gods great and small, young and old (Rig Veda 1.27.13). The number, excluding many minor deities, is in some places given as 33 (R.V. 1.34.11). In others it is given as 3339 (R.V. 3.9.9.). The total is invariably given in terms of the number 3 and in the majority of passages the numbers 3 and 11 figure prominently. On a broad survey of the Rig Veda the first impression on the mind of the reader is of the prevalence of polytheism. "Their gods are many and various. Commonly they are counted as 33; but one bold poet who gives the number at 3339 does more justice to the theopoeic imagination of his race."[3] Barnett further goes on to say:

> The Vedic religion as presented to us in the Rig Veda is not noble. Its gods are either imperfectly moralized abstractions or figures of crude humanity; even in their reverence for Varuna, the embodiment of order in the world, the poets' sense of subjection to law was far stronger than their love for the ruler and soon faded away altogether.[4]

---

[3] Lionel D. Barnett, The Heart of India (London: John Murray, 1913), p. 13.

[4] Ibid., p. 19.

Looking closely into this polytheism one notices that there are traces of early animism. But in the Rig Veda there is also a process by which a particular God is for a time regarded as supreme only to be replaced by another. He is supreme when he is worshipped by his devotees. Max Müller called this 'henotheism.'

> If we must have a general name for the earliest form of religion among the Vedic Indians it can be neither monotheism nor polytheism but only henotheism; that is a belief and worship of those single objects whether semitangible or intangible, in which man first suspected the presence of the invisible and the infinite, more than natural, more than conceivable; and this grew in the end to be an Asura or a living thing; a Deva or a bright being; an Amartys that is, not a mortal, and at least an immortal and eternal being -- in fact a God endowed with the highest qualities which the human intellect could conceive at the various stages of its growth.[5]

In other words, to all intents and purposes there is only one God to the worshipper while he performs the ceremony.

There are some who have seen in the Rig Veda progress towards pantheism or monism:

> A germ of pantheism occurs in the Rig Veda when thus the goddess Aditi is identified with all the deities, with men, with all that has been, and shall be born, with air and heaven (I.89) and in a cosmogonic

---

[5] Max Müller, *Origin of Religion* (New York: Charles Scribner's Sons, 1899), p. 245.

hymn (X.121) the creator is not only described as the one God above all gods but is said to embrace all things. This germ of pantheism developed through the later Vedic Literature till it assumed its final shape in the Vedanta Philosophy.[6]

Yet others "would see at the back of all the polytheism of the Vedas the worship of the one Triune God, Monotheism."[7]

Radhakrishnan says,

> Monotheism characterises some of the hymns of the Rig Veda. There is no doubt that sometimes the several gods were looked upon as the different names and expressions of the Universal Being. (See R.V. I.164-46 and 170-71.) But this monotheism is not as yet the trenchant clear-cut monotheism of the modern world.[8]

According to Dasgupta,

> The plurality of the Vedic gods may lead a superficial inquirer to think the faith of the Vedic people polytheistic. But an intelligent reader will find here neither polytheism nor monotheism but a simple primitive stage of belief to which both of these may be said to owe their religion ... At this stage the time was not ripe enough for them to accord a consistent and well defined existence to the multitude of gods nor to universalise them in a monotheistic creed ... It is evident that this stage can neither be properly called polytheistic nor monotheistic, but one which had a tendency towards them both, although it was not sufficiently developed to be identified with either of them. The tendency towards

---

[6] A. A. Macdonell, Sanskrit Literature (New York: D. Appleton & Co., 1929), p. 71.

[7] Srinivasa Iyengar, Life in Ancient India (Madras: Srinivasa Varadachari & Co., 1912), p. 136.

[8] S. Radhakrishnan, Indian Philosophy (London: George Allen & Unwin, Lts., 1929), Vol. I, p. 69.

extreme exaggeration could be called a monotheistic bias in germ, whereas the correlation of different deities as independent of one another and yet existing side by side was a tendency towards polytheism.[9]

There are indications in the Rig Veda of the conception of the One God in many ways manifested.

"They call him Indra, Mitra, Varuna, Agni and he is heavenly nobly winged Garutman." To what is One, sages give many a title. (R. V.1.164.46.)

To many of the singers of the Vedic hymns a species of polytheism had to suffice, but a few of them could enunciate the existence of an Unnamed, Unborn, One beside whom there is none. Man groped after God if haply he might find him. They had a vision of the One True God, but in diverse forms. It was a blurred vision. It was a shifting vision. The Vedic vision lacks the grandeur of the Hebrew conception of the One God. There is no authoritative and consistent declaration, as the Hebrew one "Hear O Israel, the Lord our God is one Lord, and thou shalt love the Lord thy God" (Deut. 6:3-4).

The Place of Siva in Vedic Religion.--Siva is not mentioned as one of the gods of the Vedic Pantheon and there is no hymn addressed to him as such. It is generally understood that Siva is known in the Rig Veda under the name Rudra.

---

[9]Surendranath Dasgupta, A History of Indian Philosophy (Cambridge: University Press, 1922), Vol. I, pp. 17-19.

> That Siva, the red god, Rudra, was an old
> Dravidian deity of South India incorporated
> into the North Indian Pantheon is, I believe,
> doubted by few ... But there is another Siva,
> the dread god of North India the son-in-law
> both of Daksa and the Himalaya, the husband
> both of Sati and of Uma (Kenopanishad iii.12)
> ... At the present time these two gods, the
> Siva of the Himalaya and He of Dravida are,
> and have been for many centuries, worshipped
> as one and the same person.[10]

The word Siva occurs in the Rig Veda as an attribute of Rudra, and means auspicious. The word also (from the Tamil) means red or gold red -- an element in the description of Siva in the Siddhanta. In the Tirivasagam Siva is "the gold red one the brightness of whose body is shaded with white ashes." (VI. line 44.) Srinivasa Iyengar thinks that the

> name Rudra meaning the Red One, seems to be
> translation of the Dravidian name Siva,
> later on adopted for the same God ... Vishnu
> and Siva were popular gods even before the
> Vedas were composed.[11]

The reason why Siva the God of the Dravidians did not find a place in the Vedic Pantheon may be due to the fact that he was the God of the defeated Dravidians. The conquering Aryans ignored the God of the conquered.

---

[10] Macdonnell, op. cit., p. 99.

[11] Srinivasa Iyengar, op. cit., pp. 125-26.

CHAPTER IV

SAIVA SIDDHANTA HINDUISM

Saiva Siddhanta is not pure philosophy nor is it a religion without a philosophy. It claims to be a 'philosophy of religion.' It is not interested in speculation on the nature of the Ultimate Reality irrespective of the reactions such speculation has on practical religion. It is concerned with a way of life one should lead for the purpose of final emancipation from ignorance and therefore claims to emphasize the more practical aspect of religion rather than the speculative aspect of philosophy.

It believes in the existence of eternal entities which are separate from one another. Siddhanta theologians take for granted certain postulates and on them build their superstructure of philosophic thought in such a way as they think will not violate the needs of everyday religion, ethics and belief in God.

Religion and Philosophy are separated in Saiva Siddhanta. Why should man reach God? If the soul is eternally and inseparably bound in Anava Mala why should it endeavor to free itself? Can the eternal bondage cease at any time? If there are three eternal entities (which we shall consider later on) later on) how can God be absolute and be Infinite without being limited by the other eternal entities -- viz. Soul and Matter? To these and similar questions the Hindu answer would be -- They are problems of philosophy and not of religion. The sole aim of religion is to point the way out of misery and ignorance and to unite man with God; and therefore it is not concerned with philosophy as such. A starving man needs only food. He does not worry himself with the botanical or agricultural aspect of rice.

Saiva Siddhanta Scriptures.--Saiva Siddhanta began to flourish as a system after the 13th century A.D. But as we have noted Saivism is pre-Aryan in origin and there are references to Siva in the Vedas. The Siddhanata theologians accept the Vedas as authoritative but they have additional books of authority. These additional authoritative scriptures are the 28 Siva Agamas which are in Sanskrit. The earliest Tamil religious writer who mentions the Agamas is Tirumular whose date is uncertain. Claims that he lived in the first century after Christ are made. He is also claimed to have lived about the 8th century A.D. The Agamas and the Saivism based on the Agamas did not originate with Tirumular; their existence is anterior to him.

The evidence of inscriptions establishes the fact that Saivism was flourishing in Conjeevaram in South India in the 6th century A.D. and that there were men proficient in the system of the Saiva Siddhantas.[1] Saiva Siddhanta theology

---

[1] R. G. Bhandarkar, Vaisnavism, Saivism and Minor Religious systems (Strassburg: Karl J. Trubner, 1913), pp. 140-43.

arose as a result of the influx of Jainism. A fierce struggle on the part of Saivism and Vaishnavism against Jainism in the Tamil country took place in the 4th and 5th centuries. So Saiva Siddhanta as a philosophical system of religion must have had its beginnings about the 4th century A.D.

So far as Tamil is concerned the Siddhanta is based primarily upon 14 treatises written by great Saivite teachers of accredited sanctity and scholarship. The 14 shastras are:

1. Sivagnana Bodham	by	Meykanda Devar
2. Irupa Irupaktu	"	Arulnanti Sivacharyar
3. Sivagnana Siddhiar	"	"
4. Unmay Vilakkam	"	Manikavasagam Kadantar
5. Tiru Untiar	"	Uyyavanta Devar
6. Tiru Kalittupadiar	"	"
7. Tiru Arulpayan	"	Umapati Sivachariar
8. Pattipaktodai	"	"
9. Vinai Venba	"	"
10. Kodikavvi	"	"
11. Unmai Neri Vilakkam	"	"
12. Sangatpa Nirakaranam	"	"
13. Nenju Vidu Tutu	"	"
14. Sivapragasamm	"	"

The authors of these 14 treatises flourished during the 13th and 14th centuries of our era. Among the 14 shastras the first place is assigned by Hindu writers to 'Sivagnana Bodham' (the teaching as to the knowledge of God) and to its author Meykanda Devar (the saint who had seen truth).

A work by Arulnanti, a disciple of Meykanda, is Sivagnana Siddhiar, the authorized commentary on the Bodham. It holds the second place among the 14 works. Of the 8 books written by Umapati the most important are Sivapragasam (the splendor of God) and Tiru Arul Payan (an exposition of Holy Grace). Umapati is the last of the four santana Acharyas (teachers in a line of succession), the others in order being, Meykanda Devar, Arulnanti and Maraignana Sambandar. These are expounders of philosophy and 'fathers of the Church' as distinguished from Samaya Acharaya, who are writers of devotional works such as Tirugnana Sambandar, Manikkavasagar Sundarar and others.

In addition to the 14 books mentioned above which are called 'meykanda sastra' there are 12 other collections known as 'Panniru Tirumuraikal.' Of these the first seven comprise Devarams of Saint Tiru Gnana Sambandar, Saint Tirunavakkarasar and Saint Sundramoorthy. The 8th collection comprises the Tiruvasakam and Tirukovaiyar of Saint Manikkavasagar. The 12th volume is the 'Periapuranam' of St. Sekkilar wherein are narrated the lives and deeds of the 62 canonised Saiva Saints. Besides these books there are other devotional literature.

Although the Saiva School of Hinduism accepts the Vedas its authoritative scriptures are the Sivagamas.

> The authoritative works on Saivism are the 28 Sivagamas which are all in Sanskrit. The truths contained in these books are believed to have come to saintly persons by spiritual illumination. The style is so terse and the meaning so abstruse, that the philosophy of these books could not be understood without extensive commentaries. A chapter (12th chapter of the 73rd section of the Pasa Vimochana Padalam of the Agama), of the Raurava Agama called Sivagnana Bodham and consisting of 12 couplets said to have been revealed to the great Saiva Saint Nandi, as the essence of the Agamas, was translated into Tamil in the 12th century by Meikandar who also added to it a commentary. This was expanded by his disciple Arulnanti in his Sivagnana Siddhiar.[2]

---

[2] S. Shivapadasundaram, *The Saiva School of Hinduism* (London: G. Allen & Unwin, Ltd., 1934), p. 16.

The teaching of the Saiva School of Hinduism got crystallized with Meykandar. Therefore it is necessary to find out if Meykandar's work is a translation of the Raurava Agama as claimed by Shivapadasundaram and the Hindus of Ceylon or if it is his original work?

> It is also wrongly believed that Sivagnana Bodham is a translation from Papa Vimochana Padalam of the Raurava Agama. Several Tamil scholars hold that the original Sanskrit sutras forming the text of Sivagnana Bodham were translated from the Tamil of Meykanda Devar and not vice versa. They all believe that the teachings inculcated in the Sivagnana Bodham were scattered here and there unknown to the multitude. Meykanda Devar collected and arranged them in a scientific form, or to use legal phraseology, codified them at a time when his fellow religionists were sunk in ignorance and troubled by internal schisms, not to speak of the extraneous influences brought to bear on their tenets by Agnosticism, Jainism and Buddhism.[3]

The argument is that Meykanda Devar collected and arranged in the form of a digest the doctrines that had existed before his time and that his codification was at a time of irreligion and of foreign influence. This compendium was the Bodham. Had Meykanda Devar been a mere translator he would have said so, particularly if he were translating a section of an Agama. It is also held that the Pasa Vimochana Padalam (section relating to the getting rid of sin) is an interpolation in the Raurava Agama and the Sanskrit version of it is a translation

---

[3]D. Gopaul Chetty, New Light upon Indian Philosophy (London: J. M. Dent & Sons, 1923), p. xviii.

of the Tamil. In the Sanskrit version the second line of the 12th sloka is capable of meaning that the first line of the sloka is from a treatise called Sivajnana Bodham. There is no such treatise in Sanskrit.

> For the sake of release, having approached the righteous, one should offer devotion to their habit and to the dwelling place of Siva; and thus understand the settled doctrines of Saivism in the Sivajnana-Bodha.[4]

Compare with this the translation of the Tamil text of the 12th Sutra:

> When having washed away the impurity which prevents it reaching the sustaining feet that are like the red lotus flower, and having joined the company of those who love the Lord, the soul is rid of delusion, it worships as Hara Himself, the habit of those who abound in devotion and his shrines.[5]

The 12th sloka in Sanskrit refers by name to the Sivajnana Bodham; the Tamil does not since it is itself the Bodham. Therefore we come to the conclusion that the Saiva Siddhanta as expounded in the 14 shastras is of purely Tamil origin and that the merit of expounding this view should be accorded to Meykanda Devar who flourished in the 12th or 13th century of our era.

As we will be considering the fundamentals of the Siddhanta in the succeeding chapters, it is sufficient to state here briefly the chief heads of the teaching of the system.

---

[4] Gordon Matthews, *Sivagnanabodham* (tr.) (Oxford: University Press, 1948), p. 82. A manual of Saiva religious doctrine.

[5] Ibid., p. 27.

God Is One. He Is the Pati -- the President or Lord.

There is not one soul but a multitude of souls which are called Pasu. God is the Lord of the souls. Eternity is postulated both of God and of souls. A soul could coexist with God as from eternity in indissoluble union, but for a third entity of which also eternity is postulated. It is Pasam, the power which keeps the soul in bondage. It is the discordant element in the soul's relationship to God. Its constant endeavor is to keep the soul apart from God. The soul would gravitate toward God but for the attraction of Pasam. The power of Pasam is wielded by Anavam (ignorance, darkness) of self assertion which prevents the soul from knowing itself and its divine affinities. Coupled with anavam are Karma (deeds) and Maya (material cause and consciousness). All souls are not subject to all the three aspects of Pasam but all are subject to anavam: some to all three; some to anavam and pasam; and others to anavam only. According to the extent of the bondage is the soul born on earth and God permits a soul to be born in a body. The soul has a capacity of becoming that to which it is attached. It is the grace of God, grace manifested to men out of compassion for souls, that frees the soul from its fetters, effects detachment, and attaches it purified to God. This union (reunion) of the soul to God is advaita -- a relationship in which God and the soul, the Pati and the Pasu, are neither one nor two nor neither. This union is attainable in this life; in the life to come it is Mukti or Veedu or Home.

This doctrine is called the doctrine of Pasu-Pati-Pasam. In the succeeding chapters we will consider them separately and in greater detail.

CHAPTER V

GOD IN SAIVA SIDDHANTA

Saiva Siddhanta teaches belief in three eternal entities known as Pati (God), Pasu (Soul), and Pasam (principle of Ignorance and Matter).

Meykanda Devar does not start with a proof of the existence of God. He takes it for granted. The summary of the first Sutra of the Sivagnana Bodham as given by Meykandar himself is: "God, who causes its Dissolution, is the Primal source of the world."[1]

This God is niskala (beyond attributes) and sakala (possessed of attributes). It does not mean that He has no attributes. But it does mean that He is beyond all attributes and qualities and is incomprehensible by the human mind. He is the Ultimate Reality. Considered ontologically God is defined as Pure Being. As such He is neither Rupi (having form) nor Arupi (formless). He is neither Chit (intelligence) nor Achit (matter). He does not create or sustain or perform other functions. Though present in and pervading all these inseparables, yet He is of a nature different from all these.

But when He is considered in relation to souls and

---

[1] Gordon Matthews, Sivagnanabodham (tr.) (Oxford: University Press, 1948), p. 7. A manual of Saiva religious doctrine.

matter He becomes the efficient cause of the Universe. His Sakti or power which is inseparable from Him is the instrumental cause.

> Sakti is the intermediate link between Siva pure consciousness and matter the unconscious ... Sakti, often called Uma, is but the reflex of Siva; and not an independent existence.[2]
>
> The attributes of God are included in Sat and Chit. God is called Sat-Chit-Anandam. Anandam or bliss is included in Chit. Hence the words Sat and Chit express all the attributes of God. Sat is Being and Chit Intelligence. The sixth sutra of Sivagnana Bodham says that if God can be perceived by the senses He becomes Asat--a thing subject to change. If He cannot be perceived in any way He becomes non-existent just like the horns of a hare. Therefore the jnanis say that He is neither one nor the other but is Siva Sat of Chit-Sat.[3]

God's functions are said to be five in number:

1. Creation, by which is meant "gift of the body and mind, of a place to live in, and of things to be known, desired and attained. The body and the mind belong to each individual. The granting of these gifts is usually called creation."[4]

2. Preservation, i.e., power to sustain the body.

3. Destruction.

4. Concealment.

---

[2]S. Radhakrishnan, Indian Philosophy (London: George Allen & Unwin, Ltd., 1931), Vol. II, p. 725.

[3]D. Gopaul Chetty, New Light upon Indian Philosophy (London: J. M. Dent & Sons, 1923), p. 9.

[4]S. Shivapadasundaram, The Saiva School of Hinduism (London: G. Allen & Unwin, Ltd., 1934), p. 60.

5. Bestowal of Grace.

Shivapadasundarum explains these as follows:

> When a person experiences pain as a result of his wrong doing, he realizes the wrongness of the action and the need for avoiding it. This realization tends to deter the man from repeating the offence, though the tendency is often counteracted by the inclination to wrong-doing due to Anavac influences. Experiencing pain is thus a twofold boon. It gives intellectual enlightenment and creates a tendency to avoid wrong doing. Similarly, the experience of pleasure which comes of doing right gives a tangible proof of the goodness of certain acts and strengthens the resolve to act similarly thereafter. The latter of the two boons is really a power to counteract the influence of Anava. These are very valuable indirect gifts of God's love received during life and may be called Enlightenment and Suppression (of Anava) respectively. These are the third and fourth gifts of God's love.
>
> The fifth gift of God's love is disembodiment or the removal of the physical body ... These 5 gifts of God's love are usually given in the following order; embodiment (also called creation), sustenance, disembodiment (death), suppression (of Anava) and enlightenment.[5]

God provides bodies and objects of enjoyment out of Maya, the principle of matter, for the souls, to enable them to get rid of Ignorance or Anava Mala.

God is the Ultimate Reality, is omnipotent, omnipresent, omniscient, eternally free from bonds and absolutely different from the souls and the world. "Since He causes the evolution of the universe He must be different from Maya, Soul and Anava which together form the universe."[6] Since He is the cause of

---

[5] Shivapadasundaram, op. cit., pp. 62-63.

[6] Ibid., p. 56.

evolution of the universe, He is omnipotent. "The possession of unlimited power is really the directing of the unlimited energy existing in the Universe."[7] Shivapadasundaram has a novel explanation to give of the omniscience of God:

> Since God causes the evolution of the universe, it is inferred that there can be nothing in it of which He is not aware. Therefore He is said to be omniscient. But He does not derive His awareness as we do by observation and inference. He transcends time; and the past, present and the future are equally present to Him. But omniscience really falls short of a correct notion of God; for knowing is an action and all actions imply change; whereas the idea of God implies that He is changeless. It is more correct to say that He is the source of all knowledge than that He is the possessor of all knowledge.[8]

Saiva Siddhanta asserts that the only quality of God which we can comprehend is Love and that this is the only quality the knowledge of which is of real value to us. "Therefore in unforgetting love the soul reaches the feet of Hara." (Sivagnanabodham Sutra II.) That is how the soul reaches the sacred feet of God. Tirumular in his Tirumantram says:

> The ignorant say Love and God are different.
> None know that Love itself is God;
> When they know that Love itself is God
> They rest in Love itself as God.

Manikkavasagar addressed God as 'My love and my bliss.' This infinite love makes Him assume forms and performs functions for the sole benefit and redemption of souls. But though He

---

[7] Shivapadasundaram, op. cit., p. 56.

[8] Ibid.

assumes forms He is neither Rupi nor Arupi. All rupa and arupa are forms only of matter which is objective to our senses and God can never be an object to us and cannot possess any of these material bodies or forms. When forms or appearances (avatars) are spoken of, they are not physical or material but are purely spiritual ones assumed by God because of His infinite love to souls and these forms can be perceived not by the physical eye but only by the aid of divine grace -- His grace as our eye. This eye is said to be the eye of gnana, or the internal eye.

On the subject of the relation of God to phenomena the Siddhanta understands:

1. That God is all but all is not God.
2. That God is different from all nature and from man.
3. That man is not God and does not become God.
4. That God is Being and also Love and as such is Personal.
5. That Maya is not nonexistent, nor caused from God, nor is it illusion. It is cosmic matter in the process of evolution and resolution.

But God, though He is equated with Love, is One who stands outside the life of individuals. He stands only as a spectator. No doubt it is His Love that has provided everything -- even the way of release. He has set the world in motion and it goes along. This is best summarized by Shivapadasundaram, a Hindu of Hindus, thus:

> Its conception of God is that of a supreme Being which far from being anthropomorphic or meddling with the universe from time to time, causes the evolution and the involution of the universe by means of agencies (like Kala and Niyati -- wherever mention is made in this book of God's Love doing anything, it is the ultimate agent and not as the immediate cause) -- in the universe itself -- reselbling in this respect the motion of the wheels and hands of a watch that had been wound.[9]

What is claimed to be the glory of Hinduism reduces it to a deistic theological system rather than the belief in a personal God who has dealings with his people in everyday life.

<u>Contemplation of God</u>.--But yet a great place is given in Saiva Siddhanta writings to contemplation of God. This contemplation of God is also called mysticism. Sir John Stewart Wallace in his article on "The World's Religions One in Mysticism" in the January 1952 number of the <u>Hibbert Journal</u> tries to define what mysticism is. "Mysticism is the modern European word for this high approach to God." "Between God and the Soul there is a great, though secret affinity, an affinity that each knows and that so few understand, an affinity that cannot be denied, but that cannot be fathomed."[10] On this kinship is based religion and mysticism or contemplation of God -- in its sane, sober, well-balanced aspect it is one

---

[9] Shivapadasundaram, <u>op. cit.</u>, p. 15.

[10] Francis de Sales, <u>Treatise on the Love of God</u> (London: Burns, Oates and Washbourne, Ltd. [no date]), p. 54.

one of the fruits of religion. The whole of religion is not mysticism. A man may profess and practice religion without being a mystic. Mysticism is the practice of the presence of God. A sure means of practicing such presence is prayer. Prayer when it passes beyond the stage of mere petitioning and becomes communion with God, takes one well into the experience called mysticism. There is a prayer without words, a prayer not bounded by place or time.

> We retire to God because we aspire to him, and we aspire to him in order to retire to him ... Our Soul giving itself to secret and familiar intercourse with God, will become all perfumed with his perfections.[11]

There is no monopoly in mysticism. Man is capable of religion. He is capable of prayer. He is capable of mysticism. The experience called mysticism is not for an esoteric few, for spiritual aristocrats. It is for democratic universal benefit; the most general necessary function of mysticism is to keep the eternal before us in our earthly and temporal life. This is what the Saiva Siddhanta treatises try to do:

> Divine contemplation is the highest moral lever, besides being an end itself. If we can contemplate God with all love and let His love dominate our minds, the thought of God will come to us of itself in whatever business

---

[11] Francis de Sales, *Introduction to the Devout Life* (tr. by Allen Ross) (London: Burns, Oates & Washbourne, Ltd., 1937), p. 74.

we may be engaged, sanctify everyone of our acts and make our lives sublime and holy.[12]

To achieve this end Saiva Siddhanta has introduced certain mantras or formulas for daily recitation by every Siddhantist Hindu.

> The simplest of these is AUM composed of three elementary sounds A U M with a continuation of the last sound. The continuation is split into two subtle sounds. These five sounds represent God, God's love which gives true knowledge (Parasakti), the Soul, God's love which causes evolution (Adisakti) and Anava. The same five things are represented by another Mantra consisting of five distinct letters ... They are used in two ways. They may be repeated either for contemplation or as accompaniments to some other exercise ... The contemplation attaches the soul more and more to God and draws it away from the things of the world and leads it to truth, goodness and bliss. The more often these formulas are contemplated in the right spirit, the more free one is from the deceptive nature of things as presented by the sense. The thoughts of God will dominate the mind and all the things in the world will more and more reflect God.[13]

Like most good things mysticism is liable to abuses.

1. There are professing mystics who claim to be experts and the elect.

2. The occult is associated and confused with mysticism.

3. Visions, trances, ecstasies are claimed to be essentials.

---

[12]Shivapadasundaram, op. cit., p. 65.

[13]Ibid., pp. 187-88.

    4. The sense of God's presence is identified with the presence itself.

    5. Mysticism is confused with asceticism.

    6. Self deification is mistaken for the Divine presence.

The abuse need not necessarily make the use bad.

It is also a false position to assume that mysticism or contemplation is a medium of salvation. Mysticism is not a means, most decidedly not the means of salvation. It is the name for the experience, of which there are degrees, of conscious, rational, personal relationship to God on the part of men and women who have been, or who honestly think they have been redeemed from sin. In a Christian setting this experience is that of persons who have 'passed from death to life' (Jn. 5.24; 1 Jn. 3.14), and this passage from death to life is effected by the redeeming love of the Lord Jesus Christ.

    <u>Mysticism -- Hindu and Christian</u>.--Mystical experience, the Christian can say, is the life in close communion with God of one to whom Christ, and the Cross and Calvary, and the empty tomb and the ascension heights of the glory of Olivet are intense realities. The Christian advancing in spiritual experience, stumbling often, can lay claim to know, as a fact, fellowship and communion with God and to have a foretaste of that fullness of joy which awaits all who shall be bidden to the

marriage supper of the Lamb (Rev. 19.9). Christian mysticism truly so called does not make any experience the authoritative channel of religious truth and does not go counter to historic Christianity. If love, bhakti in the language of Hindu devotees, is a conspicuous element in mysticism, then the highest point of God's love to man, and man's reciprocating love to God, is in the Cross. Christian mysticism cannot keep away from the Cross, for Calvary is the very essence of that attraction which draws all men to Christ and of that bhakti which frames itself in a burning desire to be closer to God.

The God-Guru idea is indispensable to Siddhanta mysticism. The appearance of the Guru at a certain stage in the development of the disciple marks an advance in his mystical standing. Christian mysticism is similarly unthinkable apart from Christ. The once physically manifested God-Guru, the historical Jesus Christ, is the ever present Christ of the believer. It is the distinction of Christian mysticism that the God-Guru is the soul's Redeemer.

<u>The Cross is the dividing mark between the mysticism of the Saiva Siddhantist and the Christian.</u>

In the Siddhanta conception of the God-Guru there is the element of 'kinship' with the human soul and the kinship is one of the Guru's qualifications for his office. The Divine Kinsman-Guru is best realized in the Lord Jesus Christ.

The sense of kinship is found in the word Redeemer. In Isaiah 54.5 God is spoken of as 'Redeemer and Husband.' The Hebrew word for 'Redeemer' is _goel_ which means a blood relation. It is his duty to redeem and avenge his kinsman. (Lev. 25.25; Ruth 3.12.) God becomes man's 'blood-relation' in Jesus Christ. Jesis is God, and being man's Redeemer, is his 'blood-relation.' The Redeemer God Guru idea of Christian mysticism is one of its great distinctions.

Not for others does the saint in the Siddhanta live. All his actions are for the saving of his own soul. This isolation of the Siddhanta mystic is impossible to one to whom Christ is the ideal and the rule. The true Christian mystic does not seek great things alone for himself. He lives for others. It is what he has striven to achieve for the saving and well-being of others that becomes the standard by which he will be judged at the last. (Matt. 25.44-46.) The self-saving aloofness of holy men is very defective in comparison with the impelling, compelling, constraining spirit of self-sacrifice so characteristic of Paul of Tarsus, Francis of Assisi, Francis De Sales, David Brainerd, Henry Martyn, William Law, and a host of others whose mysticism made them heroic adventurers for the Cross. Love seeks not its own, but, like light, like life, is self-diffusive.

The mystical life is a continual endeavor of the soul to conform to the image of the soul's beloved -- of being progressively transformed from glory to glory. (2 Cor. 3.18; Gal. 4.19; Eph. 4.13). It is not a fitful feeling or occasional emotion but a life, a sustained, continuous relationship progressing towards the fruition of final oneness. The Gospel way of putting it is 'abiding in God' (Jn. 15.3; 1 Jn. 2.28; 3,24), and such abiding is not an inert quiescence but active fruitful living.

'I am the vine, ye are the branches; he who abideth in me, and I in him, he it is that bears much fruit.' (Jn. 15. 5). The analogy of the vine and the branches is more consistent with practical mysticism than are the Siddhanta analogies of salt in water, flame on camphor, and iron in fire, which do not convey the conception of life while they stress on the intensity of the union. The life of union is a life of active, diffusive love, for the more any one is in union with God, the more is he filled with love. The expression called 'union' -- it is attested by Christian and non-Christian mysticism -- begins as a realization in this present life.

The attainment of the knowledge which leads to union is not a matter of formulas. Each soul's experience, and experience is highest when it is in Christ Jesus, is its best proof. The things of the spirit have to be discerned spiritually.

CHAPTER VI

SOUL IN SAIVA SIDDHANTA

By saying that it (the Soul) is not, by saying 'my body,' by knowledge of the five senses, by knowledge when they are suppressed, by the absence of feeling and activity in sleep, by knowing when caused to know, (it is proved that) there is a soul in the body which is an instrument produced by Maya.[1]

In the exposition which follows the following points are given:

1. Saying the soul is not implies that there is a soul.

2. Saying 'my body' implies that there is a soul.

3. Because there is knowledge of the five senses, there is soul.

4. Because there is knowledge during the suppression (of the senses) there is soul.

5. Because there is no feeling or activity in sleep, there is soul.

6. Because there is something which knows when made to know, there is soul.

7. In the body composed of products of Maya, there is Soul; for they have each a different name.

Shivapadasundaram sums these up in the words "The essence of all living beings is the soul."[2] The soul (pasu) is practically

---

[1] Gordon Matthews, *Sivagnanabodham Sutra 3* (tr.) (Oxford: University Press, 1948), p. 11.

[2] Shivapadasundaram, *The Saiva School of Hinduism* (London: G. Allen & Unwin, Ltd., 1934), p. 48.

the sum total of human personality, the 'self.'

The soul is an eternal being coeval with God. Tayumanavar, a Tamil Saivite Saint sings as follows:

Yet this I know

That ne'er from Thee have I been parted,
For lo, Thou livest; even so
My soul lives for ever.[3]

Further in stanza 622 he sings எனது நீ அன்று மனன் the translation of which would be "When Thou camest to being, then did I come into being." This sentiment is an echo of Sivagnanaa Siddhiar 3.7.3 and 3.4.20 where it is taught that souls are eternal and coeternal with God.

This eternal soul is not identifiable with anything else. See Sivagnana Bodham Sutra 3 quoted above. Siddhiar Sutra III 3 says:

> If the senses constitute the real soul, then why do they not perceive in sleep? Then the senses perceive one after another and each one a different sensation. You say this is their nature. But it is a defect that one sense does not perceive another sensation. What cognizes each sense and sensation and all together must be different from all these and it is the Soul. The five senses have no such cognition.

It is unable of itself to know God. "All the senses can only understand with the aid of the soul, and yet cannot know the soul; so also the soul can only understand with the grace of the Lord and yet cannot know Him." (Siddhiar III. 5)

Now the Soul, though eternal with God, is not by the circumstances of coeternity, to be considered God. It is very

---
[3] Tayumanavar, stanza 83.

distinctly taught in the Siddhanta that the soul is not God. Whatever affinities the soul may have to God, however God-like it can become, "the soul cannot become God and God does not become the soul and yet God is one with, and different from the soul." (Siddhiar III. 2.) It is taught that the soul, while it is held in the meshes of the senses and subjected to limitations of sense environments flutters about in helpless alienation from God, and without the Lord the soul is bound. The soul, because it is subjected to bonds (pasa) from eternity, is called the bound one (pasu). (Sidd. III. 4).

Now the Pasa (bonds and fetters) with which the soul is bound from the beginning form a three fold cord consisting of the strands of Anava, Karma and Maya. This triple bond is also spoken of as the triple impurity (malam) of the soul. The three constituents of pasam or malam are so connected as cause and consequence that they are not three but one.

The anavam which is inherent in the soul is believed to be an intensively minute defect or taint in the soul, minute but pregnant with immense potentialities. Anava is usually derived from Anu (atom) and Anu is synonymous with 'Soul.' The soul is called anu (atom) as its real vibhu (expansive) state is abridged by the taint Anava, which is anu (atom). Anavam is 'darkness,' 'veiling ignorance,' veiling itself and all else deceptively. Therefore the soul is the sightless foetus imprisoned unknowing in the womb of the dark anavam. It is the darkness of ignorance.

An aspect of anavam is 'ahangaram' and is in a way fiercer than anavam out of which it springs. A favorite Siddhanta analogy for anavam is dross. The 'original sin' of the Christian is 'anavam' to the Siddhantist. "Pervading through the numberless souls as the dirt in copper, anava mala withholds them from wisdom and effort and is ever the source of ignorance." (Sidd. III. 2). It is in terms of dross and copper that Sivapragasam explains anavam.

"Like the inherent taint in copper the eternal, primal, causal impurity obscures the souls intelligence." (Sivapragasam St. 20)

It is, as we have seen, Siddhanta teaching that

1. Anavam is an inherent taint of the soul.

2. It is attached to the soul from eternity.

3. Out of it springs 'ahangaram' or egoism.

4. It obscures the soul's intelligence.

5. It is darkness deceptively unseen.

6. Its power disappears from the souls finally saved.

The Siddhanta teaching as to Soul and Pasam, as to its bondage in anavam may have been an attempt to formulate a theory of 'original sin.' It may also be an effort at wishing that the history of the soul should be the history of God. But the wish is far from fulfillment because of the soul's election to differentiate itself from its affinities and to travel further and further away from its original kinship with the Divine. Anavam is the difficulty in the way; it has always been with the soul; it is in the nature of evil, something not-God. Then how could it be coexistent with the taintless 'nirmala' Deity? Siddhanta thinkers get over this situation by postulating for God 'Bethabetham' i.e., coexistence without mutual exclusion or externality as when two different things are connected inseparably like the association of ideas.

Anava, Maya and Karma are interrelated like sprout, bran and chaff in paddy -- the soul corresponding to rice. Anavam is inherent in souls, maya is external to souls. (Sidd. III.2. 81) By the influence of Maya there are manifest in a soul, when it is embodied, icha (desire), jnana (intelligence), kiriya (action). (Sidd. III. 2.83) What is Maya? "Indestructible, formless, One, seed of all the worlds, non-intelligent, all pervasive, a sakti of the Perfect One, cause of all the souls' body and senses and worlds, cause also of delusion is Maya." (Siddh. III. 2.53) Maya is thus the cause of complexity. Through Maya the anu (atom) called soul enters upon a career of almost interminable 'diversity' with the aid of the third malam Karma.

Maya is the material cause of creation.

> The Lord like a potter creates the world out of Maya as the material cause with the aid of His Sakti as the instrumental cause. All this universe is spread out and multiplied from the primal, invisible and subtle maya into visible and grosser and still grosser forms as life and body. (Sidd. III. 1. 18)

Anava occasions Maya and Maya performs its functions by means of Karma, but the first cause of all is God.

Maya is of three kinds -- sutta (pure), asutta (impure) and prakrit (gross). The process of the soul's purification is as follows.

1. God is He who has taken in hand the rescuing of souls from the toils of rebirths.
2. God is the permitter of Maya and births for the getting rid of Anavam.
3. God is the great might which causes embodiment.
4. God is the cause of attachment.
5. It is God's mercy which lets human beings go through the processes of action.
6. It is God's mercy which beholds the sufferings of souls in their bodies and considers them purificatory.
7. It is God's Sakti which makes souls eat the fruit of both kinds of Karma and on their performing good Karma, makes them enjoy the heavens of good merit in succession, till they join the company of the saints, and makes them 'balance' their deeds and attain the state of fitness for 'grace.'

In the Siddhanta teaching we see that it is God who identifies Himself with the soul to rid it of its Anavan and becomes its conqueror. The process of removal of Anavam by Maya is "just as the washerman washes all clothes by mixing with them cowdung and fuller's earth." (Sidd. III. 2.52)

The teaching that the soul is capable of partaking of the nature of that to which it is attached is the basis of a great Siddhanta truth.

> There is one characteristic definition of the soul which is brought out in Siddhanta alone and in no other school. It is the soul's power of becoming one with the thing it dwells in for the time being (body and God), and erasing thereby its own existence and individuality the moment after its union with the other and its defeat or inability to exist independent of either the body or God as a foothold or rest.[4]

> It is formless (arupa) and all pervasive (vibhu) but unlike that of Achit or matter. Its vyapaka consists in becoming one with the thing it dwells in for the time being (body or God). Its eternal intelligence and power is eternally concealed by the pasa (bondage) anavamala and hence called 'Pasu.' (Sidd. IV. 20)

The degree and extent of such participation are measured by the duration and intensity of the attachment. It is the Siddhanta teaching that the soul may, even in the human body, realize an affinity to God, a partaking of Godlikeness in the relationship which is known as Advaita. The word Advaita has not, in the Siddhanta, the same meaning as it has in the Vedanta. The word literally means 'not two.' It implies the existence of two things and does not negative the reality or existence of one of the two. It does not mean 'ekam or monism.' A unity or identity in duality is intended by the Siddhiar explanation of Advaita as being 'one with and different from.' (Sidd. III. 2.3)

The famous line of Tirumular அனைவர் வேதாந்தமும் அனாதி ஆனாலும் சித்தாந்தம் meaning "in the Vedanta teaching the soul thinks itself God; in the Siddhanta the soul realises its own individuality," is intended to indicate a crucial difference between the

---
[4]D. Gopaul Chetty, <u>New Light upon Indian Philosophy</u> (London: J. M. Dent & Sons, 1923), p. 89.

Vedanta and the Siddhanta and that difference lies in the estimate of the soul's relationship to God.

> As the soul is attached to its forms and organs (body) and is yet separate from the body, so also God is attached to the souls. Nevertheless the souls cannot become God, and God cannot become the souls. God is one with and different from the souls. (Sidd. III. 2.3)

> The knower will perceive God, by His grace, as ananya as the knower and the known are one and different and one-and-different. (Sidd. III. 6.8)

> If you regard God as not conceivable by the senses, it is of no use. If you contemplate Him as beyond contemplation ... it is a mere fiction. If you contemplate Him as yourself, it is also a fiction. Giving up these ficticious ideas of God, the only way of knowing Him is by His grace. (Sidd. III. 6.7)

Thus the Siddhanta theology is different from other teachings on the relationship between God and the Soul in some important respects.

i. The soul is not God, however much the soul may approach Godlikeness.

ii. The soul's individuality is at no stage to be deemed annihilated, however much it may progress in the relationship of being lost in God. "When 'one only without a second' is postulated, the very postulating implies that the thing postulated is different." (Sidd. III. 6.9)

iii. God's incessant association with the soul (Sidd. III. 6.9) postulates the possibility of the soul being intensely God-like.

iv. God and the soul are thus one, and different and one-and-different.

The 'advaita' relation is just as possible with God as with evil, with God as with Anava mala. The soul is capable of being in advaita relationship with any one of contraries, indeed with anything toward which attachment is possible. It is on this capacity of the soul that advaita teaching is based. This characteristic of the soul, capacity for attachment, leads to the soul being assimilated to that to which it is attached. The soul's potentialities of attachment and assimilation show themselves in a high degree in worship. And this worship is based on love. And it is because of love that the soul puts on one side all that lies between it and its beloved, then comes that stage in which the soul is "secondless." The stage of close affiliation to the Divine is reached by a process of wasting, as expressed by Mankkavsagar in the words நாம் அற்றுத் தெய்வமானோம், "we have ceased to be and are become deity" -- the process of reaching that state being described by Mankkavasagar as a gradual wearing away of self.

CHAPTER VII

KARMA IN SAIVA SIDDHANTA

Karma means 'action' and includes good and evil actions. The soul is spoken of in an Upanishad as "being overcome by the bright or the dark fruits of action and entering a good or an evil womb." (Maitr. 3.1) Karma is the fruit of action and is productive of results after death. One result is embodiment according to action. Early Upanishadic speculations as to the destiny of souls seem to indicate that in Hindu philosophic thinking Karma was associated with a soul from the moment of death. It is not definitely represented whether or no Karma is coeval with the soul in any prebodily state. Thus in the Brihad-Aranyaka Upanishad to Yajgnavalkya's inquiry "what becomes of this person, purusha, on death and dissolution," Arttabhaga's answer is "we two only will know of this, which is not for us to speak in public" and it is added "'the two went away' and deliberated. What they said was Karma, what they praised was Karma, verily one becomes good by good action, bad by bad action. Thereupon Arttabhaga held his peace." (Brihad. 3. 12.13) Eternity of Karma is not postulated. But it is claimed for the Siddhanta Divines that they built up the doctrine of Karma being coeternal with the soul, though this led to a logical difficulty. "If Karma is action, how could a soul have Karma before ever it had its body or did its first deed." The Upanishads and Buddhism deal with Karma as from a man's death and dissolution in time; the Siddhanta deals with it as from times before birth, from eternity. It is not our intention to go into this question but it is mentioned as one of the claims made by Siddhanta.

Karma means action and by extension of thought, the accumulated effect and energy of deeds may be considered under the following heads of inquiry;

1. Nature of Karma
2. The kinds of Karma
3. Karma and the Soul
4. Karma and God
5. The dissolving of Karma

1. As to the nature of Karma it is taught in the shastras; Gain and loss, pleasure and pain, honour and dishonour, all these six, become attached to a man in the womb. They manifest themselves as the result of one's endeavour. They are the result of the endeavour made in a previous birth. Result of present endeavour will be manifest in a future birth. (Sidd. III. 2.9)

As the fruits of husbandry yield us food for present enjoyment and seed for tomorrow, so also our acts account for our present enjoyment, and form the seed, the fruit springing from which will be enjoyed in a future birth. This is the eternal order of Karma. (Sidd. III. 2.12)

Karma comprises virtuous and vicious acts and their results, becoming loss and gain, and pleasure and pain. (Sidd. III. 2.39)

2. Kinds of Karma. Deeds are good and bad. The main division of Karma is into good and evil or merit and demerit. It is action that really counts in determining destiny. "Twofold works come to these souls by the Power of the Primal One; for His Power operates through twofold works, just as the protector of a city (acts) through a guard." (Sivgnanabodham Sutra 2.2)

Karma is further divided into three kinds. They are:[1]

a. Sanchitam -- store of deeds accumulated through a whole succession of infinite births. This follows the soul from birth to birth.

b. Prarattam -- fruit ripe out of the sanchitam store and inducing fresh births.

c. Agamyam -- deeds done in a given birth, and they are good (Punniyam) and bad (pavam).

What is agamyam in one birth is sanchitam for the next. There is a cyclic connection between these three kinds.

3. Karma and the Soul. The bond between the soul and Karma is from eternity. The soul is said "to eat the fruits of Karma."[2] The past Karma is eaten in this birth and the Karma of the last body causes a new body. The operations of Karma lead the soul; and limit it to genus, length of life and experience. When souls, as the result of deeds, assume any body, that body must be of some genus, have some limit of life, and experience some joys and sorrows. Death gives a

---
[1] *Sivapragasam*, Stanzas 28-30.
[2] *Ibid.*, Stanzas 28.

prolonged rest to the human monad to enable it to eat its karma in the next birth. Why should it have a next birth? Because it must eat the fruits of previous karma, and unless it does so, its anava mala cannot be removed. This latter then is the reason for reproduction.

4. Karma and God. If the soul is projected into embodiments by the sheer force of karma, what is God's position with reference to both the soul and the soul's karma? It is taught:

> The soul enjoys the fruits of karma through the Sakti (Power) of God, in the same way as a king metes out rewards and punishments ... or a physician applies remedies. The fruits cannot attach to a future birth ... of their own force. (Sidd. III. 2.4)

> The supreme Lord understands your deserts and makes you suffer pleasure or pain accordingly. (Sidd. III. 2.13)

> God in union with his Gnana Sakti causes souls to undergo the processes of births and rebirths by inducing their good and bad Karma. (Bodham Sutra 2)

> Siva makes souls eat karma and obtain liberation. The Lord cures the ills of karma by subjecting mankind to pain and pleasure. (Sidd. III. 2.34)

It is Karma that determines the number of births, but it is God who adjusts the birth according to Karma and makes the souls eat the fruit thereof. Without His divine Presence and Energy the soul cannot take for itself its own material body, and it can have no progress except when it is in conjunction with its material body. God's share in human destiny is his provision of grace. "It is thy grace that has bidden us to be bound by births because of our bondage to Karma."[3]

---
[3] Songs of Tayumanavar, no. 107.

5. The dissolving of Karma. Karma, linked, as we have seen, to the soul from birth to birth, and its operativeness overseen and directed by God, is like a running account. There are items of the account settled in one birth and some carried forward to another birth and then they are augmented by fresh liabilities. Is a balance never to be struck? Is the debt never to be cancelled? If so

> The moving Finger writes; and having writ
> Moves on; nor all thy piety nor wit
> Shall lure it back to cancel half a line,
> Nor all thy tears wash out a word of it.[4]

In India the law of Karma is sometimes taught to mean a principle in respect of the workings of which God remains an unconcerned spectator, and whose terrible processes, which perchance He may have instituted, He is powerless to prevent. In the Siddhanta theology the dissipation of Karma is contemplated:

i. The effect of a deed may be annulled by another deed, or by the hired expiatory services of other people and observance of certain rules the greater portion of the debt may be cancelled, and the residue carried forward into a future birth. (<u>Sivapragasam</u>, St. 31.)

ii. At the end of an aeon there takes place a dissolution of the universe but karma is kept alive and enters into activity in the new aeon. (<u>Sivapragasam</u>, St. 28)

iii. The Grace of God as the sun appears and sheds everywhere great light for Karma and its consequences. (Tiru Arul Payan iv. 2)

> Old karma (prarattam) disappears with the body, and karma accumulating in the meanwhile (agamyam) is burnt up by grace. (Tiru Arul Payan vi. 8)

---

[4] <u>Rubaiyat</u> of Omar Khayyam, verse 51.

But Grace does not work till the soul has been made fit for it in its fullness of time. There is a time of balancing -- 'the adjustment of both kinds of Karma.' This is mala pari pakam. Tirumular speaks of this time of balancing as that when by God's grace the soul becomes 'indifferent to deeds, has the triple mala (Karma included) destroyed and reaches God.' (Tirumantram 1527) It is this indifference to deeds, action without attachment that is known as balancing.

<u>Transmigration of Souls</u>.--The doctrine of Karma is linked to the doctrine of the transmigration of souls. The Siddhanta Divines seem to have accepted without question the theory of soul-transmigration as propounded in the Upanishads. The Siddhanta theologians have not given the world anything in lieu of what is enunciated in the Upanishads and the Brahamanas.

CHAPTER VIII

DELIVERANCE, GRACE, GURU IN SAIVA SIDDHANTA

Karma is one of the contrivances of a merciful providence for the purifying of souls. Karma is based upon a law as rigid as relentless, and if God is behind the workings of this law as Grace, then it is still his grace that sustains the law in its operations, watches its retributive processes, and, at the same time, has power to snap the cycle of samsara and effect the freedom of the fettered soul. If this were not so Karma in the Siddhanta would be the same as in non-theistic philosophies. What is Grace? The tamil word is <u>arul</u> generally understood as 'benevolence,' favour, grace, mercy and compassion. The classical 'Charis,' the New Testament 'Charis,' 'grace' has the same meaning as the Tamil Arul. As mere words Charis, grace and arul are interchangeable, and in theological thought they are not to be deprived of this commonness of significance. It is in the special doctrinal setting of each of the three words that something is found to be added to the normal contents of each. To the Christian for instance, grace, arul, Charis cannot be thought of apart from Christ, and so it is right to say that the contents of the Christian grace are not quite the same as the contents of the Siddhanta grace or arul. It is the setting that makes the difference. The same may be said of the Sanskrit 'prasada' grace, both as to its being equivalent, as a word, to Charis, or grace, or arul and yet not having the full contents of the Christian 'grace.'

The one great point of commonness between prasada, arul, charis, grace -- the obtaining of something unearned, unmerited and undemandable -- should not be obscured in any appraisement of the significance of 'grace' (arul) in Christianity and in the Siddhanta. The reason why I may not equate the Christian 'By grace ye were saved' (Eph. 2.8) with any analogous statement in the Siddhanta is simply Jesus Christ, for 'grace and truth came through Jesus Christ' (Jn. 1.19).

> The grace of God hath appeared bringing salvation to all men, instructing us to the intent that, denying ungodliness and worldly lusts, we should live soberly and righteously and in godliness in this present world, looking for the blessed hope and appearing of the glory of our great God and Saviour Jesus Christ, who gave Himself for us, that He might redeem us from all sin and purify unto Himself a people for His own possession, zealous of good work. (Titus 2.11-14.)

The true character of grace as something unearned, unmerited, is shown in many Siddhanta sayings, one of which is from S. Appar:

> "And when Thy lovers cry
> 'Forgive our sin,' great One forgiveness is Thy duty meet;
> For with Thee is great grace."[1]

2. Grace, in its operative aspect, as the energy of divine benevolence, is personified in Siddhanta theology, under the name Sakti. "God has Grace as His Sakti. Apart from this Grace there is no manifested Sivam, and apart from Sivam there

---

[1] Kingsbury and Philips, *Hymns of the Tamil Saiva Saints* (Calcutta: Association Press, 1921), p. 65.

is no Sakti." (Sidd. III.5.9.)

Grace, known thus as Sakti, is Uma, the Half of Him, and "she who abides in Siva's left side." (Sidd. III. 1.49) She is every form of divine activity. The Sakti is not many but only one. It is however differently manifested according to its divine functions. In the sphere of Life it is called Parasakti, that is God as manifested existence, and as Divine Life is manifested in creation, in providence and in Love, the Parasakti is known in its operations as Kriya Sakti, the instrument of Creation.

Jnana Sakti, the all-knowing, all-providing agency

Ichcha Sakti the desire for the welfare of all creatures.[2]
It is by 'grace' that the following among other acts are done.

1. The five-fold functioning of dissolution, creation, making souls eat the fruits of Karma, maturing of deeds and freeing from 'bonds.'

"The benefits conferred on the soul by God's love are fivefold and are intended to free it from the grip of Anava and to give it the means to make the fullest use of its abilities to know, to desire and to do."[3]

2. According to the Siddhanta, of the grace-aspects of the benevolence of Deity in action, the most noteworthy is Ichcha Sakti. It is by Ichcha, desire, longing, love, that God is closely associated with the career of the soul in every endeavour to save it for Himself.

---

[2] Siddhiar III. 1.63; Sivapragasam, Stanzas 2, 14, 15.

[3] Shivapadasundaram, Saiva School of Hinduism (London: G. Allen & Unwin, Ltd., 1934), p. 60.

The Ichcha Sakti of God is coextensive with the full diffusiveness of love in prolific expression. Its aim is to draw men into Godlikeness "that human beings may attain unto Divinity."[4] This is God's endeavour and is effected by close association with the soul in its vicissitudes. God becomes, in identification, 'the life of life,' 'the soul of soul.' It is of God thus close in manifestation that Tayumanavar says

> The witness true gives loving grace
> The guardian of my soul to be,
> And every moment does He spend
> In doing only good to me.

By His grace God makes Himself known to the soul in loving nearness of kinship. The workings of grace, of Ichcha Sakti are represented as God's incessant striving and seeking to save souls. God's quest of man is a Siddhanta belief far removed from the Upanishad speculations which are mainly along lines of man's quest for God. Tayumanavar speaks of the Divine seeking under the figure of a cow in search of her calf, and draws out the sense of the tender, solicitous motherliness of God. Though man has continually to strive yet all the while God keeps seeking the soul. Man's helplessness and God's solicitude for him are very distinctly taught in the Siddhanta. Now, this seeking of the soul by God is a truth recognized in non-Hindu religious thought. God, says the author of that grand Hebrew meditation on

---

[4] Tiru Arul Payan, 1.2.

the transcendant-immanent Deity (the 139th Psalm, v. 5) 'besettingly besieges' the soul. Here is a Hebrew song of the Divine Immanence, with its thought of a loving God in pursuit of a soul He is eager to win. With this can be compared Francis Thompson's "The Hound of Heaven." It is flight and pursuit that is the theme of St. Augustine's Confessions. God ever pursues, and in none but Christ is love's tender pursuit of straying souls so perfectly exemplified.

3. The idea of a seeking God finds in the Siddhanta its highest expression in the conception of the Guru, the spiritual instructor. "When because of the soul's meritorious practices the Primal One enlightens the Soul as a Guru also." (Sivagnana Bodham Sutra 8). The Siddhanta not only postulates a personal God, it emphasizes the necessity of God manifesting Himself to man for man's salvation. Hence the notable prominence assigned in all the Siddhanta Scriptures (as quoted above) and in the devotional literature of the Siddhanta, to the teaching about a divine Guru. The coming of God as Guru, Teacher, is taught with unmistakable insistence in the Siddhanta, in terms which lead to the inference of a Christian origin for the doctrine of the Divine Guru. The ideal of the Siddhanta, the man-becoming of God, is a very lofty one:

> The same Lord, who, never separate, was sustaining you ... appears as the visible Guru.
>
> Will any person other than intimate relations know the secret disease afflicting a person?

How can the world know Him who, without being known, came down to breathe his Grace?

The ignorant with dark thoughts cannot feel the Arul (Grace) and see the Arul-Guru.

The world cannot know that His human form, like a decoy, is assumed for snaring men.

Cease thinking, 'Of what use is He to me?' Who can learn anything as the Shastras themselves require the Divine Guru. (Tiru Arul Payan v. 1-6)

Here we have one of the great books of the Siddhanta declaring:

1. That God must needs come to men as the Guru, for even the old scriptures require His illumination.

2. That God, as such Guru, assumes forms.

3. That the God-Guru is One who knows the infirmities of human nature, as an intimate relation knows the secret disease. This last is not merely a reason for God's becoming-man but a requisite in the God-Guru, so that He might be in sympathy with the soul's infirmities. The Vedanta abridges all distance between man and God by its equation "I am God." The Siddhanta more rightly, and consistently with its environments of the Rig Veda and Brahmanic Avatars, enunciates the man-becoming of God as a preliminary to the possibilities of the God-becomingness of man. The Vedanta postulating identity of essence, takes a leap from manhood into the Godhead; the Siddhanta interposes the man-becomingness of God between man and man's Maker. Man is not God, it says, God is not man, yet God assumes the form of man that He may teach men the secret of The Grace which is to give men the means of attaining the fullness of the stature of God-likeness.

At first the Siddhanta ideal may seem to stand in the place of the Christian view of the Incarnation. In reality it is not so.

1. The avatars and other appearances of God in the Hindu Books are only forms. The Siddhanta lays stress on the forms assumed by God. These manifestations are not incarnations, just as the theophanies of the Old Testament were not.

2. In forms, the ideal, to have a Guru who will know the soul's disease, is imperfectly realized. In the Incarnation alone is the Ideal fully realized. That God took on Him the nature of man, and the form of man is Christian teaching. This is the furthest point of God's manbecomingness.

3. The Siddhanta will not have the idea of God being subjected to the limitations of birth and death.

We have in the New Testament, without a doubt, the last word on the man-becomingness of God. The revelation is there of the Word made flesh (Jn. 1. 14), of God taking upon Himself not the nature of superhuman beings but of man (Heb. 2. 16), that He might sympathize with human infirmities (Heb. 4. 15) as an intimate relation knowing one's secret disease, and be an intercessor encompassed with and subject to man's limitations, 'tempted in all points like as we are, yet without sin."(Heb. 2.18; 4. 15). The New Testament thus fulfills the prophetic foreshadowings of the religions of the world, and affords the only adequate realization of the Siddhanta ideal of the God-Guru. How full this realization is may be seen by the fact of God being declared born for men, a very man, and dying for men, so that the man-become God should not escape the last limitation of man, death. One appreciates the hesitancy of the Siddhanta to accept the teaching of a God born to die, but such hesitancy need not exist when the New Testament triumphantly asserts from the first (1. Thess. 4. 14 and Acts 2. 32), that Jesus Christ rose again from the dead. The New Testament not only speaks the last word on the man-becomingness of God, but it has the last word on the God becomingness of man. Jesus Christ died to enable man to be dead to sin (Rom. 6. 2-11) and He rose again from the dead to enable man to rise with Him. (Rom 6.4; 14. 9; 4.24) Again, "We all, with open face beholding as in a glass the glory of the Lord, are changed into the same image from glory to glory" (2 Cor. 3. 18; cf. Col. 3.4).

"Now we are the sons of God, and it doth not yet appear what we shall be, but we know that when He shall appear we shall be like Him, for we shall see Him as He is." (1 Jn. 3. 2)

This is the New Testament idea of the God-becomingness of man, this is man's certain hope, and the hope prompts him to practical preparation (1 Jn. 3.3; Col. 3. 1, 2, 3) for the abundant life in God, for the life that now is and for the life that is to be. Man realizes in this life the beginnings of God-becomingness, for the Model Man, the Lord become Man, the Divine Guru in whom are fulfilled all God's promises to humanity, has given the soul this assurance; "Abide in me and I in you. As the branch cannot bear fruit of itself, except it abide in the vine, no more can ye except ye abide in Me." (Jn. 15. 4)

The God-Guru idea is foreign to the Upanishads. It is possible however, to trace in the Upanishads the suggestion of material out of which has been evolved the God-Guru conception of Siddhanta theology. It is necessary, says an Upanishad, for the seeker of knowledge to become the disciple of a Guru who is 'learned in the scripture.' A Guru is necessary since 'knowledge learned from a Guru best helps one to attain his end.' These references are to human instructors. However suggestive these may be it is held that in the Upanishads we do not discover the full fledged God-Guru idea which one meets in the Siddhanta teachings.

The Siddhanta Divines expressly teach that God manifests Himself as the Guru, (Sidd. 3. 8.1; Bodham 8; Tiru Arul Payan v. 1), grants His Grace (Sidd. 3. 12.6) and liberates the mature soul from future births and anava mala (Sidd. 3. 8. 10).

As a type of the uniform teaching of the Siddhanta doctors that Siva becomes Guru, may be mentioned the clear and unambiguous teaching of Tirumular in Tirumantram No. 1573 following:

> God Himself is the Saiva Guru
> It is God the Omnipresent who is the taintless Guru.
> He who is above all the worlds, the holy Siva, is in this world the praiseworthy holy Guru.
> The Holy Siva becoming the Guru.

What then is the form in which God manifests Himself to men? Souls by reason of their eternal attachment to anava mala have the substance of the bodies for them evolved out of maya but God not being subject to anava mala, the 'substance' for His body, in assuming human form, is evolved out of His Sakti and not out of maya. According then, to the Siddhanta, the form assumed by God is a non-material, spiritual one, somewhat akin to the docetic body ascribed to Christ in early Christian heresy.

God so highly conceived may be born, may graciously assume a body, may take on human name and even live within the limitations of human history, but he does not see death. Every endeavour is made by the Siddhantists to avoid entertaining, even in the very least possible degree, the conception of a dying God. They concede that the birthless One may be born a man but they decline to carry the incident of human birth and human existence to the point of death. Now, the Siddhanta does not deny to Deity the capacity for complete man-becoming, since it teaches 'It cannot be postulated that He is this and that He cannot become this and that.' (Siddhiar 3. 1. 44). In other words 'with God nothing is impossible.' (Luke 1, 36). The Siddhanta theologians lived in the Christian era, long after the Christian teaching of a dying God, dying to rise again from the dead, had found its way into Tamil India and it is possible that because of knowledge of such teaching, they, while conceding to their God-Guru some degree of humanity, recoiled from postulating of his death. We must recognize in the Siddhanta a likeness to the Christian conception of the God-Guru. On the other hand, the insistence of Siddhantic scholars upon the man-becoming of God as something phantasmic, makes the cleavage between the two conceptions, the Christian and the Siddhanta very wide indeed. Into the mouth of the God-Guru according to Christianity the words could truly be put, "A body hast thou prepared for Me" (Heb. 10. 15), a body, as distinguished from a docetic semblance of a body. In addition to two points of difference between the God-Guru conceptions,

1. the God-Guru's body, in Christian thought, is a real human body, and not a 'form,'
2. the God-Guru in Christian thought, is one tasting the uttermost bitterness of the ills of human life, death,

we have on this matter of a dying God-Guru, a further and striking mark of difference,

3. the God-Guru's dying is the furthest humanly conceivable reach of the love of the Deity, for 'greater love hath no man than that he should lay down his life for his friend.' (Jn. 15. 13.)

The idea of a dying Christ is not the mere idea of a man dying for his friends; it is the sign of the uttermost stretch of God's love for souls. 'God so loved the world that He gave His only begotten Son that whosoever believeth on him should not perish but have everlasting life.' (Jn. 3. 16) The cross is an offense to the Siddhanta as it was a stumbling block to the Jews and foolishness to the Greeks. (1 Cor. 1. 23). The Siddhanta has no cross -- it is lacking in the highest possible proof of Love that will go the length of sacrificing itself for the sake of sinsick peoples. The Cross is in the very heart of

God. It is the fibre and essence of Love; God is Love. Love can never love fully, if it cannot sacrifice freely.

The Siddhanta conception of the God-Guru, in spite of its sublimity, and its uniqueness in Indian religious thought, and indeed, in spite of the grand inspiration it has given the Siddhanta saints for a passionate, personal love for God, however named, lags considerably behind the Christian idea. The most vital difference is the Cross which is to the Christian the high watermark of the love of God. Love that, remaining sinless, dares 'becoming sin' (2 Cor. 5. 21) for sinners and tastes death for them has reached the uttermost limit of sacrifice.

CHAPTER IX

LIGHT AMIDST DARKNESS

We have seen in our study that amidst the seeming polytheism of Saiva Siddhanta there is a strong undercurrent of monotheism. God is a personal God with whom man has to unite. The expectation of a Guru or a Teacher, the righteous one, the Perfect, -- of God Himself coming down amongst men as such a One-Guru -- is an outstanding feature in Saiva Siddhanta literature. A very learned Hindu's comment on this belief in God becoming Guru is significant both for its language and its Christian colouring:

> Unless God comes down to us as the Son of Man our redemption is not possible. Christianity speaks of only one revelation for all time to come, but in the Saiva Siddhanta God reveals Himself as Son and Guru to each in his own fullness of time.[1]

The conception of the Incarnation, though not of the character of the fact of 'God made flesh' is yet lifted far above the conception of avatars.

The Saiva Siddhanta teaching of the saving Arul (Grace) of a personal God has relieved the doctrine of Karma of some of the rigours of the Vedanta teaching. The Siddhanta doctrine is in a Christian atmosphere. "The doctrine of grace, a special feature of the Siddhanta, differs in no respect from that of the

---
[1] J. N. Nallasamipillai, *Studies in the Saiva Siddhanta* (Madras: C. Coomarasawmy & Sons, 1909), p. 299.

Christian doctrine."[2] (But we have noted the difference in our study in Chapter 8). The same writer finds in Jn. 15; 4-6, teaching which he thinks is in accord with his religion and which dispels the gloom of the inexorable workings of Karma.

The parallels in teaching between Christianity and the Saiva Siddhanta reveal that there has been light amidst the darkness. Hinduism is not all ignorance and superstition and darkness. But even amidst its darkness there is a light -- even if it be a faint light at times. The light shineth through the darkness. But the claim of Christianity is that Jesus Christ is the only True Light that lighteth the world.

<u>How can we account for this Light in Hinduism?</u>--

1. We must gladly confess that God has never left Himself without witness (Acts 14. 17), that the illumination of the Spirit is without respect of persons (Acts 10. 34), and that verily there is a Light that lighteth every person that cometh into this world, (Jn. 1. 9).

By saying this we are not relegating the religion of Christ to an undistinguishable commonness. To the Christian his religion is not so much a man's quest for God, as God's quest for man. Sufficient is revealed to him to guide him aright along the path of salvation, yet much remains unrevealed. The secret things belong unto the Lord our God but those things which are revealed belong unto us and to our children that we may act.

---

[2] Nallaswamipillai, <u>op. cit.</u>, p. 355.

(Deut. 31. 29). Christianity is catholic enough to recognize that in every nation he that feareth God and worketh righteousness is accepted with Him (Acts 10. 35), and is at the same time consistently uncompromising enough to insist that "there is none other name under Heaven given among men whereby we must be saved." (Acts 4. 12) The Christian is not driven to an attitude of toleration and recognition toward other faiths than his, by anything that has happened in recent years. From the earliest times the duty of the Christian has seemed clear. Augustine laid it down "Whoever is a good, true Christian, let him recognize that truth wherever he may have found it, belongs to his Lord." Justin Martyr claimed that whatever things have been rightly uttered in all places are the property of us Christians.

To the ignorant and bigoted, Hinduism is on the same footing as any form of fetishism, and Hindu worshippers of wood and stone, the workmanship of their own hands. To think so is to shut one's eyes to much that is great and noble in Hinduism. The ethnic faiths were the preparation for the religion of the greatest of Asiatics, Jesus the Nazarene. They had to exhaust their possibilities before the fullness of time could come, for the self-manifestation of God to man. They are part of the Divine discipline by which the race of man has been tutored and trained for the requirements of a fuller revelation. Many non-Christian faiths have been as darkness before the dawn, others as the dawn before the daylight and the thoughts of their making as the songs before the sunrise. Rightly has it been said "The pre-Christian religions were the age long prayers and the Incarnation was the answer."[3]

2. God reveals Himself directly and indirectly by various kinds of influences. We have noticed that the Saiva Siddhanta began to flourish during the 13th century and onwards. Looking back into the history of Christianity in India we find that there are evidences of Christianity in South India even from the first century of our era. The Syrian Christians of South India claim that their Church was founded by the Apostle Thomas himself. "The apocryphal Acts of Thomas and their continuation, The Martyrdom of Thomas, both probably dating from the second half of the third century, recount the missionary labour of the Apostle Thomas in India."[4]

Even if this is not accepted as historically true and verifiable there is evidence that Christianity was in India very early.

> About the year 180 says Eusebius in his Church History, there were still many evangelists who sought to imitate the godly zeal of the apostles, by contributing their share to the extension and upbuilding of the Kingdom of God. Among these was Pantaenus, who is reported to have reached the Indians amongst whom he is stated to have found the gospel of St. Matthew which, prior to his arrival, was in the possession of many who had known Christ.[5]

---

[3] Lionel D. Barnett, *Bhagavad-Gita* (London: J. M. Dent & Sons, 1928), Introduction, p. 3.

[4] Julius Richter, *A History of Missions in India* (tr. by S. H. Moore) (London: Oliphant Anderson and Ferrier, 1908), p. 27.

[5] *Ibid.*, p. 28.

We find again, "Among the 318 Bishops who took part in the Council of Nicea, there was a certain John Bishop of all Persia and Greater India."[6]

Cosmas Indicopleustes, who journeyed in the Indian waters in 530, refers very briefly in his writings to Christians in Ceylon and India.

> What I have seen and experienced in the majority of places during my stay I truthfully declare. On the island of Taprobane (i.e., Ceylon) in Inner India, where the Indian Ocean is, there is to be found a community of Christians consisting of both clergy and the faithful, but I do not know whether there are any Christians to be found beyond this. Similarly in Male (Malabar) and in Kalyan near Bombay, there is also a Bishop who receives imposition of hands from Persia.[7]

There is evidence of Christianity in India until about 850 and then for four centuries nothing is known -- from 850-1250. But yet Marco Polo, who traveled in the East from 1270 to 1295, mentions that "in the kingdom of Quilon (Travancore) dwell many Christians and Jews who still retain their own language."[8] Marco Polo further relates the martyrdom of Thomas and tells of his body lying in a shrine. Tradition ascribes Madras as the place where his body lay. So that this goes to prove that Christianity was practiced from Madras right down to the southern tip of India. So it can be inferred that Christianity had been exerting its influence on the life and

---

[6]Richter, op. cit., p. 29.

[7]Ibid., pp. 31-32.

[8]Ibid., p. 38.

thought of India and it is safe to assume that the Saiva Siddhanta Santana Acharyas were influenced in their thinking by Christian doctrines.

3. A third factor which must be borne in mind is that there was trade and commerce between India and the Ancient World from time immemorial. Srinivas Iyengar proves from quotations and other evidence that South India had trading connection with the outside world starting from Babylonia in the fourth millenium B.C. Coming to the Christian era he says, "The trade grew to such enormous proportions in the time of Claudius and Nero (54-68 A.D.) that Pliny complained in 70 A.D. that India drained gold to the value of nearly a million pounds a year -- 'giving back her own wares which are sold among us at fully a hundred times their first cost.'"[9]

He goes on to describe how this trade continued even up to the times we are interested in.

Greek and Roman coins dating to these periods have recently been unearthed in South India.

This evidence of contact between the peoples of the earth -- India and the world outside -- resulted in a mutual give and take of goods and ideas and of religious thoughts and beliefs.

This interchange is found even in the Old Testament. Caldwell, in his Grammar of the Dravidian Language, records many words that have passed into Western languages. The things

---

[9]Srinivas Iyengar, The History of the Tamils from Ancient Times (Madras: C. Coomarasawmy Naidu and Sons, 1929), p. 305.

listed in 1 Kings 10. 22 include the Peacock and Ape as well as ivory, silver and gold -- all of which are indigenous to India. The Hebrew name for peacock is undoubtedly derived from the Tamil. The Hebrew is 'tuki' while the Tamil is 'tokei' which sometimes appears as 'tukei.' Caldwell goes on to say that it is from this root that the Arabic 'tawas,' the Greek $\tau\alpha\acute{\omega}s$ and ultimately the Latin 'pavo' and the English 'peafowl' are all derived.

In both the 9th and 10th chapters of 1 Kings we are told that Solomon had a navy and that it sailed from the Eloth on the Red Sea to Ophir and Tarshish. A great deal of conjecture has gathered round the words Ophir and Tarshish. The expression 'ships of Tarshish' does not mean ships going to, coming from, made at or harboured in any place called Tarshish but 'a large class of vessels similar to those which went to Tarshish'; a 'certain class of specially strong and large ships destined for longer voyages.'[10] [11] If so, 1 Kings 9. 22 does not mean an expedition to Tarshish or that 'ivory, apes and peacocks' came from Tarshish. One fact is indubitable, viz., that Solomon's 'ivory, apes and peacocks' came from a Tamil country to judge from these Tamil names preserved in the Hebrew.

4. Hopkins in 'India Old and New, pp. 120 to 169

---

[10] J. C. Hastings (ed.), *A Dictionary of the Bible*, Vol. IV (New York: Charles Scribner's Sons, 1908), p. 804.

[11] *Ibid.*, p. 684.

discusses the many parallels in teaching and legends between Christianity, Buddhism and Hinduism and ends this section by saying,

> The little band of early Christians in South India may have been instrumental in fashioning the lofty ideals of some of the noble religions which we know existed in after time and the influence of which in their turn may still be potent among the sects of today. That there was a late counter growth from seeds of the Orient, which, starting in India, blossomed in the Occident in tales of saints and in moral legends, found first in Persia, then in the Talmud, and finally, perhaps, in the vision of Dante may be admitted. The West owes much to India, and though most of this was brought westward centuries after the Christian era, it is still within the bounds of possibility that even the New Testament was not completed without a graft from such a foreign growth.[12]

The Hindus date the present era of the world from the time of the Deluge called Jalapralayam. They recognize four ages of the world. Each age is called a Yuga. The first stage lasted 1,728,000 years; the second, 1,296,000, and the third 864,000 years. We are now in the last stage which is called the Kali Yuga, the age of misery. This age should last about 432,000 years -- the year 1953 being the 5,054th year in the yuga. At the close of each of the yugas there took place a universal upheaval in nature. No trace of the preceding age or yuga survived in that which followed.

> The Kali Yuga dates from about the same time as the epoch of the Deluge -- an event clearly recognized by them and very distinctly

---

[12] E. W. Hopkins, India Old and New (New Haven: Yale University Press, 1913), p. 168.

mentioned by their authors, who give it the
name of Jala pralayam or the Flood of Waters.
Their present era, indeed, dates specifically
from the commencement of this Jalapralayam.
It is definitely stated in the Markandeya
Purana and in the Bhagavata that this even
caused the destruction of all mankind, with the
exception of the seven famous Rishis or Peni-
tents ... who were saved from the universal
destruction by means of an ark, of which Visnu
himself was the Pilot. Another great Personage
called Manu, who as I have tried elsewhere to
show, was no other than the great Noah himself,
was also saved along with the seven great Peni-
tents. The Universal flood is not, to my knowledge, more clearly referred to in the writings
of any heathen nation that has preserved the
tradition of this great event, or described in
a manner more in keeping with the narrative of
Moses, than it is in the Hindu books to which
I have referred.[13]

There have been other versions of the Deluge given by various peoples. Skinner in his Commentary on Genesis in the International Critical Commentary series discusses the Deluge. He comes to the conclusion that there could not have been a universal deluge.[14] What we are concerned with here is not the truth or falsity of the occurrence of the Deluge but of the prevalence of a tradition about the Deluge. The Deluge may be legendary, or mythical. But the Babylonians, the Greeks, the Jews, the Egyptians, Persians, Indians, Syrians,

---

[13] Abe J. Dubois, Hindu Manners, Customs and Ceremonies (tr. by Beauchamp) (Oxford: Clarendon Press, 1906), pp. 416-17.

[14] John Skinner, A Critical and Exegetical Commentary on Genesis (New York: Charles Scribner's Sons, 1910), pp. 174-181.

Phrygians, Phoenicians, all refer to a Deluge. This parallel account of the Deluge and other parallels in teachings of various religions make us infer, though not positively nor conclusively, that there may have been a common source of tradition for all the peoples of the earth.

At any rate, God has not left Himself without witness at any time, and through trade and commerce there was widespread dissemination in the ancient world of religious beliefs and teachings.

But Jesus Christ is the final and ultimate revelation of God. In our final and concluding chapter we will consider this claim of Christ -- Jesus Christ the Light of the World.

CHAPTER X

JESUS CHRIST THE LIGHT OF THE WORLD

In our study we have come to the conclusion that there has been light amidst the darkness of Hinduism. I agree with Farquhar when he says "for we hold Him to be the Light which lighteth every man and we believe that even in the savage minds God left not Himself without witness and that the very lowest men show the pith of the law written in their hearts."[1] But I do not agree with him when he says "He is the crown of the faith of India."[2] Light is basically the same. But yet candle light and electric light are not the same. They are both light but yet they are different. Electric light is not the fulfillment of candle light. Nor yet is electric light the fulfillment of Sun light. The difference between Christianity and other religions "lies in another direction than that of grade or richness of religious experience."[3]

What then is the difference between Hinduism and Christianity? What is it that the Christian has which the Hindu has not? Three of the most vital things may be noticed.

1. Jesus Christ
2. The Church
3. The Bible

---

[1] J. N. Farquhar, *The Crown of Hinduism* (London: Oxford University Press, 1915), p. 2.
[2] *Ibid.*, p. 458.
[3] H. Kraemer, *The Christian Message in a non-Christian World* (London: Harper & Brothers, 1938), p. 285.

I. <u>Jesus Christ</u>.--The Hindu religion is not founded by any single person. It has no founder as the Buddhist, the Mohammedan and the Christian religion has. The Hindu has no message of universal import to proclaim. His is an individual solitary effort to work out his own salvation. But Christianity has a message to proclaim. It is the proclamation of an event -- the event of God's coming down in Jesus Christ as the Lord of all Life and as the Light of the world. In this proclamation three things are implied.

a. That God became man in Christ Jesus that sons of men may become sons of God. "God sent forth His Son, born of a woman, born under the Law, to redeem those who were under the Law, so that we might receive adoption as sons." (Gal. 4; 4-5)

b. That in Christ we receive the new birth, the forgiveness of sins and the gift of the Holy Spirit. "In Him we have redemption through His blood, the forgiveness of our trespasses, according to the riches of His grace which He lavished upon us." (Eph. 1; 7-8)

c. That Christ is the King of this world of ours. That it is His reign now. But when He shall have subdued all God's enemies then will the Kingdom of God come in its fullness. "Then at His coming, comes the end, when He delivers the Kingdom to God the Father that God may be everything to every one."(I Cor. 15. 24, 28)

Through this event Jesus Christ the Incarnate Son of God

reveals (1) God to man. He reveals God not as a synthesis of all that is beautiful; not as the highest concept that man can have; not that God is an object of thought to be analyzed and discussed. But that He is the One with whom man has to deal -- that He is the Living God -- independent of all our thought about Him. He is the God who meets man in personal encounter. He is the God who belongs to persons. He is the Eternal Thou.

(2) This Eternal Thou is the Creator. Almost all religions accept God as the Creator. The Creator God of the Christian is different from that of the non-Christian. To the Saiva Siddhantist Hindu God is the first cause, the un-caused cause, the unmoved mover who has set the world in motion like a clock maker or a cosmic engineer. (See above, p. 34) But the Christian conception of God as Creator is different. God is not pensioned off as in the other religions. Christianity speaks of the Creator and creaturehood and not of Cause and Effect. In the Christian conception there is a continuing relationship between the Creator and the created. Everything is dependent on Him and everything is derived from Him. The world *is*, because God wills it. It is not a machine world left to carry on by itself. God is in dynamic relation to His creation, like an artist, always engaged in that which He is creating.

(3) God is a God who redeems. The concept of a redeeming God is foreign to Hinduism.

Christ proclaims that God has done for man and to man what he could not do for himself. He is a God who *does*, not simply a God who *is*. In Hinduism God *is*. He has life and He is the source of life. But He is not a God who *does*. He is not a Redeemer-God. Man has to work out his salvation through countless number of births and deaths.

To a Christian the phrase 'living God' does not mean a God who has merely life but it means a God alive in history. Consequently history takes on a new meaning. What Jesus meant by 'My Father is working still and I work' (Jn. 5. 17), is that God is active in history for redemption. God active in history for redeeming man is unique in Christianity.

This raises the question why does God redeem? In Genesis 9, 8-13, we have the story of the rainbow. The rainbow is set as a covenant between man and God that there will be no further destruction. God is betrothed to humanity and because He will not destroy He must redeem. The throne of God is set beneath the rainbow. (Rev. 4. 3) God's covenant is to redeem. Redemption is God working in history.

This raises another question: What does God redeem man from? To the Hindu man has to be redeemed from Anava Mala or Ignorance. But to the Christian redemption is from Sin.

In the view of the Bible Sin is an intrusion into human nature. Man is a creature made by God and made uniquely in His image. He is a creature but not a mere creature as an animal for he is capable of being addressed by God and is answerable to God. According to Brunner:

> ... the Christian faith asserts that we can only understand him in the light of the Word of God ... but we mean something far more fundamental, namely, that the way of human existence, the being of man itself, that in which it is different from all other forms of being, can only be understood in the light of its relation to the divine Word, namely, as being in the Word and from the Word of God .... Human existence, in contrast to every other form of existence, is responsive existence, that is, existence which must and can answer, and in so doing is free and yet bound.[4]

Responsive awareness of God is the unique thing in man. This is not an extra added to him. This is the truest thing about Him. This is what makes him man. Man in God given design is a creature designed for God. But something has happened. Man is wandering. God's design is shattered. What shatters the design is not Ignorance or Anava Mala as in Hinduism but Sin. Sin is an intrusion into human nature and an incursion into God's world. Man must be set free from Sin. Sin is slavery of the soul and not a mere disease of the soul. Sin is a rebellion. It is a refusal to live according to God's design. Sin is a master whose wages is death. (Rom. 6. 23) Sin is an entity (Jn. 7. 7). "Whatever views a person may hold on this subject, he may as well face the fact that the question of his Satanic Majesty, the Devil, has been reopened in the thought of our time."[5] Whether we

---

[4] Emil Brunner, <u>Man in Revolt</u> (Philadelphia: Westminster Press, 1947), pp. 64 and 65.

[5] John A. Mackay, <u>God's Order</u> (New York: The Macmillan Company, 1953), p. 29.

accept the presence of the devil or think of the 'principalities and powers' of Paul we are led to the conclusion that Sin is an entity to be contended with. I find that I am not antiquated in my belief for I find that an eminent scholar like Mackay saying the following:

> A very real aspect of the Rift which cleaves the Universe is the presence of inexorable Forces or Powers of an impersonal character which affect terrestrial life and frustrate human aspiration. Even should the view be taken, which I believe to be philosophically unwarrantable, Biblically unsound, and religiously perilous, that there is in the Universe no personal power of evil, there still remain 'things in heaven'; Principalities and Powers. These forces, however they may be interpreted in their ultimate nature, are realities to be reckoned with in history, because human history is in many crucial respects controlled by them.[6]

Sin thus we find is a human predicament, and not a mere proneness. Sin is there and has to be dealt with. God has dealt with Sin by dethroning it. God came down in Jesus Christ and dealt with Sin on the Cross. Jesus has revealed that the initiative for man's redemption is wholly from God. "And as Moses lifted up the serpent in the wilderness, so must the Son of Man be lifted up, that whosoever believes in Him may have eternal life. For God so loved the world that He gave His only Son that whoever believeth in Him should not perish but have everlasting life." (Jn. 3. 14-16)

This redemption in Christ is made available to everyone

---
[6] Mackay, op. cit., pp. 32-33.

who believes on Him right now. It is not something to be obtained in the distant future. It is immediate. He has paid the price. By dying on Calvary He has taken upon Himself the consequences that otherwise according to the law of Cause and Effect, would have befallen us. Our Karma is broken. He has bought us with the price of His own life, and by paying the price due to death, He has made us His property and as Paul says we are bondservants of Christ. We were condemned to die but Christ has redeemed the pledge by paying the price.

Sin today is prowling about like a beast with a mortal wound inflicted on it, but it is not dead yet. But God's Victory will be complete when Sin is completely destroyed. (Rev. 19. 20) When Sin and Death are no more, then Redemption will be complete. God has dealt with Sin. He now deals with the sinner.

Jesus Christ declares God as Redeemer-Creator. The awareness of God as Redeemer is prior to awareness of God as creator. The logical order and the Hindu order is to go from creation to redemption. But the Christian order is from redemption to creation. The Redeemer is Creator. The Redeemer-Creator gives the assurance that He is man's Saviour. This is what made Paul exclaim 'I know whom I have believed' (2 Tim. 1-12).

The story of redemption is that man is truly human only when he is united to God. He is not human in his lost state, when he is away from God and is not united to Him. Redemption is the Divine pouring Himself into man. This is the experience of abiding in Him, of being hid in Christ.

The Incarnation is a movement of God towards man. He came down not to give imperishable maxims -- the world had already had such maxims -- He came to destroy Sin and to give eternal life to man. The redemptive rule of Christ in history began with His Incarnation. The Son of God has appeared to destroy the works of Evil and to make men the sons of God.

Christ's work is a decisive, unique, once-for-all victory over Sin and Death. His Incarnation, ministry, special works of Power, Death, Resurrection and Ascension, all together make up an organic unity and form one unified form of action which accomplished salvation. God in Christ has dealt with Sin. Sin has received its mortal blow. Having dealt with Sin on the Cross, He deals with people now.

That is the Gospel which the Christian has which no one else has. The Christian message is 'News' -- news which means something new, something that has never happened before.

It is 'good news' because God has come down to redeem man. An end for man's quest for God has come. All religious quests center round the question of the right relationship between God and man. The Christian Gospel -- the good news -- is that 'Christ is the Christian answer to the age-old problem of right relationship between God and man.'[7]

---

[7] W. M. Horton, *Our Eternal Contemporary* (New York: Harper & Brothers, Ltd., 1942) p. xviii.

God's love works. Jesus Christ is here. Jesus Christ is there. God in Christ is our Eternal Contemporary. Jesus is Leader, Saviour and Victor -- Then and Now.[8]

II. <u>The Church</u>.--To the Hindu, life is a life lived in community, where every individual and every group had a part to play. Dillistone quotes from p. 367 of Radhakrishman's <u>Eastern Religions and Western Thought</u>,

> Individuals and classes were bound to one another by what is called the spirit of status and not terminable contract. Every man had his place in society and fixed duties attached to it. The social organism expected from each man his duties but guaranteed to each subsistence and opportunity for self expression. The spirit of competition was unknown.[9]

Again Dillistone quotes from a Western scholar from p. 101 of <u>J. H. Hutton's Caste in India</u>,

> The caste system afforded a place in society into which any community, be it racial, social, occupational or religious, can be fitted as a cooperating part of the social whole, while retaining its own distinctive character and its separate individual life.[10]

It is not the intention of the authors cited nor is it my intention to uphold the evils of the caste system particularly the treating of certain sections of humanity as untouchables. But the point brought forward is that all life has to be lived in community. The Hindu community life is a social community life. The life of the community as such has no

---

[8] Horton, <u>op. cit.</u>, pp. 34-123.

[9] F. W. Dillistone, <u>The Structure of the Divine Society</u> (Philadelphia: Westminster Press, 1951), p. 16.

[10] <u>Ibid.</u>, p. 17.

religious emphasis. It has no corporate religious life. Religion is an individual matter. Each one has to work out his own salvation. No doubt at certain times and seasons of the year, crowds will gather together in Temples at Festivals and in pilgrimages. But this does not give them a solidarity in worship. There can be an individual Hindu but in Christianity there can be no individual Christian. Because he is part of a religious community. The Christian community life is of an entirely different type. The Christian community we refer to is the Church. Four main differences may be noticed. (a) It is a convenanted community. "In the Old Testament the spiritual relationship between God and Israel is conveyed by one word, so constantly repeated as to be in many ways the key word of the Old Testament revelation, the word 'covenant'."[11] The Church is the result of a covenant God made between a particular man and a woman -- Abraham and his wife. The whole story of Israel is looked upon as a fulfillment of this covenant, God ruling and overruling when this covenant was broken or about to be broken, till in Christ a new Israel is formed with a new covenant. All through the Bible the central theme is this covenant of Redemption. Redemption is God working in us and for us until we turn to live in Him. "I will betroth thee unto me for ever; yea, I will betroth thee unto me in

---

[11] Stephen Charles Neill, The Christian Society (London: Nisbet and Co., Ltd., 1952), p. 7.

righteousness and in judgment, and in loving kindness and in mercies; I will betroth thee unto me in faithfulness and thou shalt know the Lord." (Hos. 2. 19-20) God is wooing His bride the Church to be faithful to Him.

> Christ's intimate relation of love to His Church, His solicitude for its beauty and holiness, the Church's duty of responding in reverent subjection to her Lord, -- these are deductions drawn from the Church's status as the Bride of Christ. Nowhere in the New Testament is organic imagery so clearly interwoven with covenantal. It is, in fact, within the family circle that the most adequate picture of the Church of Christ is to be found.[12]

The Church is set up by Christ. It is not a human organization nor a social set-up. We do not make a Church but we are born into it (Heb. 3. 6), 'We did not choose Him but He chose us.' (Jn. 15. 16)

"In the New Testament the Church, the ecclesia, is the community consisting of those whom God has called. The sole foundation of the Church is the will and choice of God; God, not man, is the auctor ecclesiae."[13]

(b) This community is the Body of Christ. (Eph. 1. 15-22) Paul hints that Christ is incomplete without a Church in which God's love can operate and manifest itself. The Church is Christ's Body the final perfection or fullness of Him who filleth all in all.

---

[12] Dillistone, op. cit., p. 69.
[13] Emil Brunner, The Divine Imperative (Philadelphia: Westminster Press, 1947), p. 524.

He, then, in whom dwells all the fullness of the Godhead bodily, in turn fills His Church with the fullness of life which He himself is ever receiving from the Father. This life is a life of $ἀγάπη$, of sacrificial love. It is in being united with Christ in His suffering and death that the Church becomes filled with all the $πλήρωμα$ of God.[14]

(c) The Church is a community which is possessed by the Holy Spirit. What happened at Pentecost was the giving of God's gift of the community -- the Church. The reality of brotherhood of man is realized because it has found fatherhood in God. A brotherhood built without God ends in confusion. That is the story of Babel. But Pentecost is God's answer. The people at Pentecost spoke one language -- the language of the Holy Spirit. The Church belongs to God through the Holy Spirit.

The Church is the place where the triune God -- God the Father, God the Son, God the Holy Spirit is at work.

(d) The main function of the Church as the Body of Christ is to make man meet God in Christ in the Divine-human encounter as happened at Caesarea Phillippi. "Who say ye that I am"? is the question and the answer "Thou art the Christ." God in the person of Jesus Christ meets person in Peter and vice-versa. The task of the Church is to put the world in the krisis -- to make people encounter God in Christ and help them to make the confession as Peter did.

---

[14] Dillistone, op. cit., p. 67.

Because the Church stands to Christ as a temple to its foundations, as a body to its head, as a bride to her husband, therefore the inference is drawn, not that the Church's nature is of a particular kind, not that its structure is of a particular pattern, but rather that its duty is to behave in a particular way, its privilege to receive the grace which will enable it to fulfill its particular destiny in the high calling of God in Christ Jesus its Lord.[15]

III. <u>The Bible</u>.--The first affirmation about the Bible that has to be made is that it is one book and yet it is not one book. It is Τὰ βιβλία, the books. More than two thousand years had elapsed between the time of the patriarchs mentioned in the first book of the Bible and the time of the writer of the last book of the Bible. More than 750 years had elapsed between the writing of the first and last books of the Bible.

In it we find many assortments; myths as in Genesis, chapters 1-4; legends of the great heroes of the past as Samson; facts of past as seen through the haze of the past; history as in Samuel and Kings; Philosophy as in Deuteronomy; collections of Laws as in Leviticus; wedding songs as in Song of Solomon; funeral hymns as in Lamentations; moralistic philosophy as in Proverbs and Ecclesiastes; religious drama as in Job; hymn singing in Psalms; sermons in Prophecies; the Gospels have the good news and the Letters the reflections on the good news. Amidst all this diversity, the Bible is

---
[15] Dillistone, <u>op. cit.</u>, p. 69.

one Book because of one subject. It deals with the activity of the living God. It is this which gives authority to the Bible. It is this which distinguishes it from the sacred books of other religions.

The narratives in the Bible are not meant as moral lessons. The Hero of every Bible story is God. It is not man but it is the living God who is the Hero of the Bible. Every event in the Bible deals with the activities of God.

> We note finally that the Bible, as witness to God's revelation, testifies to his person and to his great acts. The Bible is no communication of 'timeless or eternal truths' complete in themselves, but always a 'kerygmatic' word, demanding to be proclaimed in its saving dynamic. For this proclamation is a part of God's word. It is always the Living God addressing himself to man.[16]

Conclusion.--The Christian has a story to tell to the nation -- a message to proclaim to the whole world. That "Christ descended that the Church might ascend seeking those things which are above where Christ sitteth on the right hand of God."[17]

> A Church that believes in its mission must proclaim to him as to all men throughout the world Jesus Christ, Lord and Saviour, who transforms man and society, through whom God is reconciling the world unto himself, Jesus, Lord of this world and beyond, Lord unto eternal life.[18]

---

[16] Richardson & Schweitzer (ed.) *Biblical Authority for Today* (Philadelphia: Westminster Press, 1952), p. 85.

[17] Dillistone, op. cit., p. 68.

[18] Sabapathy Kulandran, *The Message and Silence of the American Pulpit* (Boston: The Pilgrim Press, 1949), p. 139.

"Arise, shine; for thy light is come; and the glory of the Lord is risen upon thee." (Isa. 68. 1)

"The Day Spring from on high hath visited us." (Luke 1. 78)

"Now unto Him that is able to keep you from falling and to present you faultless before the presence of his glory with exceeding joy, to the only wise God our Saviour be glory and majesty, dominion and power both now and ever Amen." (Jude 25)

BIBLIOGRAPHY

BOOKS:

Barnett, Lionel D. Bhagavad-Gita. London: J. M. Dent and Sons, 1928.

_____. The Heart of India. London: John Murray, 1913.

Bhandarkar, R. G. Vaisnavism, Saivism and Minor Religious Systems. Strassburg: Verlag von Karl J. Trubner, 1913.

Brunner, Emil. Man in Revolt. Philadelphia: Westminster Press, 1947.

_____. The Divine Imperative. Philadelphia: Westminster Press, 1947.

Chetty, D. Gopaul. New Light upon Indian Philosophy. London: J. M. Dent & Sons, 1923.

Dasgupta, S. A History of Indian Philosophy, Vol. I. Cambridge: University Press, 1922.

Dillistone, F. W. The Structure of the Divine Society. Philadelphia: Westminster Press, 1951.

Dubois, Abe J. Hindu Manners, Customs and Ceremonies. Tr. by Beauchamp. Oxford: Clarendon Press, 1906.

Farquhar, J. N. The Crown of Hinduism. London: Oxford University Press, 1915.

_____. An Outline of the Religious Literature of India. London: Oxford University Press, 1920.

_____. A Primer of Hinduism. London: Oxford University Press, 1912.

Finegan, Jack. The Archeology of World Religions. Princeton: University Press, 1952.

Francis de Sales. Introduction to the Devout Life. Tr. by Allen Ross. London: Burns, Oates and Washbourne, Ltd., 1937.

_____. Treatise on the Love of God. London: Burns, Oates and Washbourne, Ltd. [n.d.].

Hastings, J. C. (ed.). *A Dictionary of the Bible*, Vol. IV. New York: Charles Scribner's Sons, 1908.

Hopkins, E. W. *India Old and New*. New Haven: Yale University Press, 1913.

Horton, W. M. *Our Eternal Contemporary*. New York: Harper and Brothers, 1942.

Iyengar, Srinivas. *The History of the Tamils from Ancient Times*. Madras: C. Coomarasawmy Naidu and Sons, 1929.

_____. *Life in Ancient India*. Madras: Srinivasa Varadachari and Co., 1912.

Kingsbury and Philips. *Hymns of the Tamil Saiva Saints*. Calcutta: Association Press, 1921.

Kraemer, H. *The Christian Message in a non-Christian World*. London: Harper and Brothers, 1938.

Kulandran, Sabapathy. *The Message and Silence of the American Pulpit*. Boston: The Pilgrim Press, 1949.

Macdonell, A. A. *Sanskrit Literature*. New York: D. Appleton and Co., 1929.

Mackay, E. *Early Indus Civilizations*. London: Luzac and Co., Ltd., 1948.

Mackay, John A. *God's Order*. New York: The Macmillan Company, 1953.

Macnicol, N. *The Living Religions of the Indian People*. London: Student Christian Movement Press, 1934.

Marshall, J. H. *Mohenjo-daro and the Indus Civilization*. London: A. Probsthain, 1931.

Matthews, Gordon. *Sivagnanabodham*. (Tr.) Oxford: University Press, 1948.

Müller, Max F. *Origin of Religion*. New York: Charles Scribner's Sons, 1899.

Nallasamipillai, J. N. *Studies in the Saiva Siddhanta*. Madras: C. Coomarasawmy & Sons, 1909.

Neill, Stephen Charles. *The Christian Society*. London: Nisbet and Co., Ltd., 1952.

Pope, G. U. *Tiruvachagam*. (Tr.) Oxford: Clarendon Press, 1900.

Radhakrishnan, S. *Indian Philosophy*, Vol. I. London: George Allen & Unwin, Ltd., 1929.

―――――. *Indian Philosophy*, Vol. II. London: George Allen & Unwin, Ltd., 1931.

―――――. *The Hindu View of Life*. London: George Allen & Unwin, Ltd., 1927.

Richardson and Schweitzer (eds.). *Biblical Authority for Today*. Philadelphia: Westminster Press, 1952.

Richter, Julius. *A History of Missions in India*. (Tr. by S. H. Moore.) London: Oliphant Anderson and Ferrier, 1908.

Shivapadasundaram, S. *The Saiva School of Hinduism*. London: George Allen & Unwin, Ltd., 1934.

Skinner, John. *A Critical and Exegetical Commentary on Genesis*. New York: Charles Scribner's Sons, 1910.

PERIODICALS:

The Hibbert Journal, January, 1952.

ARTICLES:

Encyclopedia Britannica, Vol. XII. Chicago: Encyclopedia Britannica Inc., 1952.

DATE DUE

PRINTED IN U.S.A.

CPSIA information can be obtained
at www.ICGtesting.com
Printed in the USA
FFHW011251250119
50322073-55374FF

9 780957 025127